ENEMY IN THE SHADOWS
The World of Spies & Spying

NORMAN GELB

First published in the United Kingdom in 1976 by William Luscombe Publisher Ltd

This edition published in 2018 by Sharpe Books.

ISBN: 9781726864152

CONTENTS

For my father.

INTRODUCTION

Some years ago, when I was broadcasting from Berlin for an American radio network, I had lunch from time to time with a man I shall call Josef, a correspondent for the news agency of an East European country. Josef believed I was an American spy and I was certain he worked for Russian intelligence, either directly or through his own country's espionage service. We used to joke about our mutual suspicions.

He was a jolly, thoroughly entertaining fellow and our lunches were enjoyable encounters during which we spoke openly and jocularly about our conflicting political beliefs and our differing assessments of political developments. Josef was, in fact, the first Communist I had met who could treat ideological differences with anything other than stodgy, overbearing ponderousness.

One day, he told me he was studying Spanish because he hoped to be assigned by his news agency to Cuba where he said, with a seriousness that occasionally crept into our sessions, he hoped to observe the 'brave revolution' that was taking place under Fidel Castro. Jokingly, and with no 'inside' information whatsoever, I suggested that he study hard and learn Spanish quickly because the Cubans, I said, are a volatile people and it was possible that Castro would soon be overthrown, 'maybe even tomorrow'.

The next day, the abortive invasion of Cuba at the Bay of Pigs, organized by the American Central Intelligence Agency, was launched, became the focus of world attention, and changed things between Josef and me. From that moment on, the mood of our lunch meetings was transformed. He remained friendly, but the light-heartedness was gone forever. Josef appeared convinced that I had tried to give him advance warning of the Bay of Pigs operation and that, because of the levity which characterized our luncheon chit-chats, he had not seen through the camouflage obscuring my discreet tip-off.

There were to be no more jokes, no more banter. He would not be found less than vigilant again. At our subsequent meetings, he posed an awkward succession of obviously prepared, earnest questions on political, economic and military subjects and listened carefully to whatever answers I could muster. Reluctant to end what had been an enjoyable relationship, muster them I did, rehashing stuff I had written for broadcast or read in the press. To make matters worse, Josef took to retiring to the men's room with improbable frequency, I assumed to make written notes, not trusting his memory.

The episode was absurd. Indeed many of the incidents which occur in the world of spying are equally absurd and just as devoid of cosmic significance. The extent of time and energy devoted to tracking down and evaluating insignificant snippets of information is breath-taking.

Nevertheless, espionage, as an instrument of national policy to which extravagant efforts and resources are devoted, is, for the most part, a serious undertaking. Despite its often futile pursuits and activities, it has had far-reaching consequences over the course of history. It is, for example, impossible to overlook or dismiss the decisive influence on the Second World War of intelligence operations which gave the British access to German military communications (and affected all major military confrontations on the western front and Africa) and which gave the Russians access to Japanese strategic plans (allowing them to shift desperately needed armies from their eastern borders to help stop the German advance across the Russian heartland).

Though dramatic and intriguing, espionage, like war, is immoral. Like war, it has a long and fascinating history as well as a complex manual of procedures, both of which this book attempts to explore.

1. THE SPY AND HIS CRAFT

Hero or villain, success or failure, the spy has always been a figure of excitement and mystery. He has always occupied a zone of shadows. He has always had a reputation, not always earned, for living on the brink of exposure and personal disaster, a tightrope walker without a net, a pilot without a fuel gauge.

In a world which professes moral standards, the spy is an unnatural creature. He exists in a realm of guile, duplicity and intrigue. The terrain he scours is pockmarked with plots, tricks, conspiracies and stratagems, mostly of his own making. His tools include deception, manipulation of confused loyalties, exploitation of human weaknesses, burglary and, occasionally, murder. His *modus operandi* is abominable by any ethical standards. Whatever acclaim he may receive from those who believe in the cause he serves, and however evil he may consider those he betrays or deceives, his personal behaviour is that of a scoundrel; it contributes to the awesomeness of his calling.

The spy may be a patriot, serving his country; or he may be what is commonly deemed a traitor, serving another country because of what he considers a higher loyalty. A choice few have been major historical figures, perpetrating acts of momentous significance. Most have been — and are — diminutive cogs in biggish wheels, performing relatively minor roles, making small contributions to ambitious espionage operations which proved to be (or not to be) of great (or limited) importance. For many, the effort, risks and stratagems have been ultimately futile, based on misconceived, wretchedly executed or basically hopeless planning.

A person becomes a spy for any of a complex variety of reasons. He may be motivated by patriotism, political conviction, ideological commitment, money, love or fear. He may be drawn in by a web of psychological inducements: the craving for adventure, a search for power, the thrill of living a double life, the challenge of avoiding detection, or the prospect of manipulating situations and people. Some are military men assigned to espionage as others are assigned to the artillery.

Some spies are temporary agents, flirting with or inveigled into espionage for brief periods or isolated operations. Others bring intense, almost pathological devotion to the causes they serve. Oleg Penkovsky, who employed his position as a colonel in the GRU (Soviet military intelligence) to feed secrets to the West, continued to do so in Moscow even after he knew his cover was blown and that his arrest and doom were imminent. The American revolutionary war spy, Nathan Hale, when caught and condemned by the British, regretted only that he had but one life to give for his country. Unbidden, the Persian, Zopyrus, slashed off his own nose and ears to convince the enemy Babylonians that he had been mutilated and disgraced by his own people. It was an extreme, but successful ploy to gain the sympathy and confidence of besieged Babylon so that he could open its gates to the waiting Persian invaders.

Fear was the spur for Colonel Alfred Redl, a homosexual Austrian general staff officer, blackmailed by the Russians into handing over vital military secrets immediately prior to the First World War. In the Second World War, some British subjects of German ancestry were compelled by threats to relatives still in Germany to serve the German espionage apparatus — though British intelligence was able to convert most of them into useful double agents.

Disappointment and vengeance have also propelled men along the path to espionage. Swedish Colonel Stig Wennerstrom, imprisoned in 1964 for betraying his country's military secrets to the Russians, was bitter about having been passed over for a promotion he had confidently expected and badly wanted.

The spy has been around a long time. He appears in the Old Testament and in historical tales recounted by Herodotus. His function was well known in ancient China. Long before fiction conjured up the mythical trench-coated, two-fisted secret agent, karate-chopping and blasting his way to the most guarded secrets of enemy powers, espionage had developed into a subtle, intricate art and a complex system of skills.

Ideally, espionage operatives should be imaginative, resourceful and skilled at their craft. Their qualities should include audacity, courage, perseverance, patience, self-control, resilience, a sharpened sense of timing and, above all, good judgment. Many of the great spies of history have displayed these characteristics. But there have also been spies and spy masters who were incompetent, plodding and downright dense.

The East German intelligence official who planted Communist spy Gunther Guillaume in West German Chancellor Willy Brandt's personal staff should have known that Brandt, who was getting along very well with the Communist regimes of eastern Europe for policy reasons of his own, would have been furious if he knew about Guillaume (Brandt resigned in 1974 immediately after Guillaume's arrest and West Germany's attitude toward the Communist countries stiffened). Nor can one envy the CIA agent whose activities in Singapore were exposed when his electrical apparatus blew the fuses of a local hotel, an incident which enraged the otherwise pro-American Singapore President Lee Kwan Yew.

A successful agent must, of course, be able to conceal his identity. Colonel Rudolph Abel, a Soviet military intelligence officer, inconspicuously ran a Russian network in North America for several years while posing as a professional photographer in New York. He was caught only after being betrayed by a disgruntled subordinate who tended to be careless and impunctual and who was exceedingly fond of hard drink — hardly the mental make-up of a successful spy. He was en route back to Moscow, summoned home to answer for his shortcomings, when he defected and provided the American authorities with enough information to track Abel down.

Catalogue of Jobs

There are several kinds of espionage operatives. The category which most stirs the popular imagination is that of secret agent in the field, the undercover spy. He is known as an 'illegal'. He is an outlaw, subject to arrest and imprisonment, and sometimes still to torture and execution.

But most espionage operatives spend their working days in tranquil, undramatic circumstances, in offices in their own countries or in their own embassies in foreign lands, never exposed to danger. They perform espionage functions which are widely understood and more-or-less accepted by everyone concerned. They include the headquarter troops of the espionage war, the planners, supervisors and evaluators. Abroad, they are often shielded by diplomatic immunity.

In recent years, a new breed of spy has emerged — the pilot of high-flying reconnaissance planes and crew member of spy vessels, equipped with sophisticated equipment for monitoring installations, movements and communications of adversaries from relatively unchallengeable vantage points.

Though some have been the centre of ugly international incidents, they are usually tolerated grudgingly by those they spy upon, provided they do not intrude on territory of countries equipped to detect them.

Spies have, from time to time, engaged in acts of sabotage, destroying enemy supplies, disrupting enemy logistics and undermining enemy morale. Such operations, usually undertaken in wartime, are invariably dramatic and have sometimes lent meaningful support to military operations. But their significance is usually minor when compared with the actions of armed forces. The dynamiting of a weapons warehouse is simply not in the same class as, for example, a high-powered military assault or an effective bombing raid.

Similarly, such acts of violence as murder and kidnapping are usually of limited or transient importance as espionage operations. An anti-Communist journalist was murdered in Afghanistan after ignoring warnings that he would be silenced unless he stopped writing about Soviet espionage activities in the Moslem world. The anti-Soviet feelings aroused by his death balanced out any gains the KGB (Soviet Committee for State Security) may have derived from eliminating him. Russian-born British agent Sidney Reilly was implicated in plans to assassinate Lenin and disrupt the new Soviet regime shortly after the Russian Revolution. His webs of intrigue, highly spiced with audacity and daring-do, produced no memorable results other than some good anecdotes and a subsequent suggestion that he had ended up working for the Russians. (The world of espionage lends itself to that sort of speculation.) The American Central Intelligence Agency developed such an indelible reputation for cloak-and-dagger rashness that it was often said to be responsible for even the natural deaths or misadventures of those who seemed ideally suited to be CIA victims. Subsequent disclosures during the course of congressional investigations that it had in fact plotted the assassination of some foreign leaders (notably in Cuba) came as no surprise.

The occasional murder of a spy by a rival secret agent was, until recently, a recurring theme, particularly on mutually foreign ground. But, to sustain the morale of their men in the field, espionage agencies were increasingly compelled to demonstrate that they valued their lives enough to take vengeance. There were, as a result, some angry shoot-outs between western and Communist agents in Vienna and Berlin after the Second World War. But gang warfare, especially in other countries, exceeded what national agencies could long tolerate and it was phased out by all parties concerned. When a senior officer at a Soviet military mission in West Germany (a tolerated spy, just as western missions in East Germany were staffed by tolerated spies) was run down by a car in Frankfurt in 1960, it was feared the Russians would consider it an assassination and that the shooting would erupt again. However, Moscow was finally persuaded that it had been an accident and not covert action on the part of western agents.

It is *covert operations* that have given espionage its reputation for Machiavellian plotting. They involve secret, aggressive actions, including so-called *dirty tricks*, to damage an adversary. A dramatic, if obvious, example was the incident at the German town of Gleiwitz on the Polish border the day before the Second World War started. A group of Polish-speaking German agents, dressed in Polish Army uniforms and carrying Polish weapons, attacked the Gleiwitz radio station, beat up its German staff, made a virulent anti-German announcement over the radio and left. Though Hitler was determined to start the war in any case, the incident, immediately publicized widely throughout Germany, enraged Germans and helped prepare them for the attack their armies were to make on Poland the following morning.

More subtle and of greater significance was the British planting of the 'man who never was' on German intelligence prior to the Allied invasion of the Continent in Normandy five years later. The body of a man who had died of pneumonia was given a new identity through forged papers, decked out in a British officer's uniform, and forged documents indicating clearly that the Allied assault would take place in southern Europe rather than Normandy were put in a briefcase chained to his wrist. The body was then put into the sea off the Spanish coast by a submarine, but was made to appear to have come from a plane crash. As expected, the Spanish authorities who recovered it let the Germans examine the documents and the body before returning them to the British. As a result, a German military build-up in southern Europe diverted forces which might otherwise have reinforced those thrown against the Allied invaders.

An argument can also be made for considering the case of the Trojan horse, described by Homer, as a highly successful exercise in covert operations, leading to the fall of Troy. But, to be precise, the Greek act of building the huge, hollow wooden horse was merely a diversionary military ploy. The dirty trick at the heart of the operation must be credited to Sinon, the Greek prisoner who convinced the Trojans that not to drag the horse — and the Greek soldiers concealed within it into Troy would offend the goddess Athena.

More recent covert operations have been equally laden with intrigue. They include KGB deception of the leaders of the Hungarian revolt against Russian rule in 1956 which led to their capture and execution after they had received false assurances that Russian occupation troops would be withdrawn from their country, the tunnel the CIA dug from West Berlin to East Berlin in the early 1950s to hook successfully into the telecommunications system of Russian Army headquarters in East Berlin, and the success of Soviet military intelligence in recruiting Portuguese army officers in the early 1970s to prepare the way for an attempted Communist putsch in Portugal.

Dirty tricks include compromising and blackmailing foreign officials, often through threatening to expose sexual deviations or more conventional hanky-panky. A French ambassador to Moscow was trapped by the KGB in the late 1950s when a KGB agent, pretending to be an irate Russian husband, found the diplomat with his 'wife' (an agent whose friendship with the ambassador had been meticulously nurtured by the KGB). The 'husband' beat up the ambassador, who went running to Russian (KGB) officials for help in hushing up the embarrassing affair. He was assured that there was nothing to worry about. But the Russians planned to blackmail the ambassador, for whatever services he could perform, after he returned to Paris to take up a senior government post there. Their plot was foiled when a KGB officer, involved in the charade, defected to the West and told all. The compromised ambassador was quietly put out to pasture.

Disinformation has been a particularly effective form of dirty trick. It is the dissemination of false information about an adversary. Though recent hostility between India and the United States has geo-political origins, much of its element of bitterness can be traced to Russian forgeries of publicized letters purported to have been written by American officials, seeming to indicate that Americans were totally insensitive to India's potentially disastrous food shortage, despite vast American aid to India. The CIA has engaged equally energetically in the practice of disinformation, notably in documents it forged implicating the Russians in plots against the Peking government. Chinese-Russian antagonism later became so dangerous without outside assistance that American policy changed and efforts to widen the rift were dropped.

2.   THE PRIMARY ASSIGNMENT

Despite the adventure and intrigue of covert operations, by far the most important function of espionage and of secret agents is not planting bombs or rumours, or eliminating or compromising individuals. It is gathering information, compiling 'intelligence'. Even for espionage purposes, intelligence covers a comprehensive spectrum of knowledge, ranging from easily obtainable facts and opinions to the most closely guarded secrets. It can be classified in four major categories: general, political, strategic and tactical.

1 *General Intelligence* deals with such matters as a country's topography; the character of its shores, beaches and tides (if it borders the sea) and of its rivers and other inland waters; details of its economy and of its transportation and communications systems; the character of its people; and a wide range of other general areas of information. With the help of general intelligence, Bismarck's Prussians knew every step of the way when they overran France in the 19th century. The Allied landings in Normandy, which marked the beginning of the end of the Second World War, were preceded by the most thorough study of the French coast ever undertaken.

Much general intelligence is now readily available in standard reference works, including almanacs and better tourist guides. These days, the libraries of major national intelligence services have immense files containing answers to most possible questions of general intelligence, relating to potentially hostile, and even friendly, countries. They are kept up to date by intelligence officers posted under legitimate diplomatic cloak to the countries in question. An awareness of the potential significance of general intelligence explains why maps, timetables and similar generally innocent documents, so easily obtainable in many countries, are hard to come by in Russia, China and other xenophobic lands.

2 *Political Intelligence* is, similarly, often an open book in most countries. It concerns the various political forces at play in an adversary nation, and in friendly nations too. It records potentially differing aspirations and goals of different political movements and personalities within a country and the possible impact such differences might have on political decisions. Such knowledge could be of vital significance in times of confrontation. For example, when Gerald Ford was about to succeed Richard Nixon as president of the United States in 1974, the Soviet Union wanted advance knowledge of the extent to which Ford was likely to maintain Nixon's east-west detente attitudes, a subject of great importance in the formulation of Russian military and diplomatic policies. Information the United States acquired about Saudi Arabia's reluctance to join most other major oil producing nations in squeezing western economies helped formulate America's assessment of the ability of the West to ride out the oil crisis.

Concerned foreign governments invariably prefer to know in advance what course new regimes are likely to follow after political changes take place, either through elections or coups such as those which have altered the policies of Greece, Chile, Algeria, Iraq, Indonesia and other countries in recent years. Information about the imminence of a coup obviously can be of some value to countries with interests at stake, even when the scope of their possible response to the situation may be limited.

Political intelligence increasingly concerns itself with

economic matters of international consequences. The development of movements among Third World countries favouring the emergence of cartels to control price and supply of raw materials is of profound concern to industrial countries. As suggested above, the oil panic of the 1970s put pressure on national espionage agencies to probe the factors which would influence oil producing nations to alter oil prices and rate of production. A dramatic failure of intelligence was highlighted by the Soviet success, in 1972, in secretly buying up a good part of America's grain reserves at bargain prices — purchasing from several American grain merchants while keeping each in the dark on the magnitude of overall Soviet grain needs and purchases. A coup of major proportions, it was a great embarrassment to the American government and has led to intensified efforts by American intelligence to keep watch on Russian agricultural production, and the Russian economy in general.

In most countries, the gathering of political intelligence is totally respectable. Political and commercial officers at embassies read local journals and other relevant literature and maintain contact with government officials and other leading personalities who are in a position to offer information, freely and innocently, or to influence their government's policies. Aside from immediately useful knowledge thereby obtainable, today's parliamentarian, congressman or political party functionary could be tomorrow's government minister and should be cultivated. Planning for the future is an important aspect of political intelligence work. Diplomats engaged in gathering such intelligence sometimes maintain contact with locally-resident exiled political personalities who might one day return in triumph to determine the policies of their own countries.

3 *Strategic intelligence* is essentially what this book is

about. It has been the province of the great spies of history as well as of most other, less illustrious, secret agents. It is the stealthy extraction of usually guarded national secrets which can be of specific use to a potential or actual enemy. It concerns diplomacy, long-term military strategy, weapons development and, increasingly, classified technological information concerning, for example, nuclear and industrial research.

The Russians fielded several networks in Britain and the United States simultaneously after the Second World War in a frantic effort to obtain western atomic secrets. The Americans recruited disillusioned and disgruntled officials and military officers in Russia and East Europe to keep tabs on military developments in the Communist world. Both made wide use of their diplomatic services to further their espionage objectives. Napoleon's agents penetrated the courts of adversary kingdoms to assess the various forces contesting his control of Europe at the beginning of the 19th century. Elizabeth I's spies kept watch on the Spanish as they prepared the Armada that subsequently tried and failed to destroy England's sea power.

Strategic intelligence also covers less spectacular ground. It can, for example, deal with such matters as the acquisition of secrets of weapons-purchasing contracts between other countries and details of differences within policy-making groups of a rival nation. Much more significant is the development of spy-in-the-sky earth-orbiting satellites capable of probing major strategic secrets, including the development and positioning of intercontinental missiles.

Though the acquisition of strategic intelligence can be difficult and dangerous, it is sometimes as easy to come by as political and general intelligence. The Institute of Strategic Studies in London openly publishes periodic assessments of comparative military strength. A high ranking Polish espionage officer who ran a spy network while stationed in Washington as a diplomat for his country said, after he had defected to the West, that though much of the information fed to him by his agents was valuable, among his most important sources had been American scientific and technical journals on sale, then as now, on newsstands.

4 *Tactical intelligence* concerns a very specific arena — that in which military actions are played out. It covers details of military deployment, tactics and weaponry under actual warfare conditions. It involves the dispatch of agents — usually military personnel — through enemy lines to acquire the desired information. It also involves the use of agents-in-place, recruited before the event or when needed, often members of resistance movements in areas occupied by foreign forces. Things being what they are in war, tactical intelligence spies are often shot or tortured when captured. If heroism can be defined as the ability to live under the shadow of death or the prospect of intense pain, they are the heroes of the world of espionage.

The purpose for which tactical intelligence is gathered is obvious. Detailed knowledge of the strength and positions of opposing forces can greatly assist a military commander in planning either offensive or defensive operations. So can awareness of how much of what kind of weapons and other supplies the enemy can count on.

All wars involve the deployment of tactical intelligence agents, sometimes only as patrols or scouts, but often as down-to-earth spies. Until American forces in Vietnam tightened base security, spies who infiltrated their headquarter installations obtained information about planned operations, permitting the Communist Vietcong, against whom the operations were designed, to withdraw or lay ambushes well before the Americans went into action. British, French and other Allied spies in German-occupied Europe during World War Two transmitted coded radio messages which directed bombers to German military, transportation and industrial targets. *Evaluation of Intelligence*

Although potentially of great value, capable even of turning the tide of battle, tactical intelligence, like everything else, is worthless if improperly exploited. Military commanders, required to make urgent, important decisions, frequently distrust or do not have time for reports from spies. German intelligence chief Walter Schellenberg complained bitterly after World War Two that Hitler often refused to act on reports from secret agents which detailed Allied military movements and which later were proved to have been accurate. Similarly, Stalin often ignored information from Russian spies, including advance word of the date of the German invasion of Russia in 1941.

Agents in the field can do no more than gather intelligence. The task of evaluation and subsequent action falls to their superiors. Modern espionage agencies have large evaluation sections in which reports from the field are assessed in the light of various considerations, including the reliability of the agent's past performance, the likely accuracy of the report in view of reports from other sources, prevailing conditions, and the possible consequences of courses of action that could be taken as a follow-up to the report.

Israeli spies reported strong Egyptian and Syrian military build-ups prior to the attack on Israel in 1973, but their superiors, much to their subsequent regret, concluded that the reports were overblown and decided against a major defensive build-up of their own. American navy intelligence intercepted and deciphered Japanese code messages early in December, 1941, which indicated that a major move by Japan was imminent; nevertheless, the American fleet in Hawaii was unprepared for the Japanese attack on December 7th. On the other hand, American U-2 spy planes took photographs which revealed that the Russians were installing nuclear missiles in Cuba, 90 miles off the Florida coast, in 1962. This information prompted the United States to take action which forced the withdrawal of those missiles. During the Cyprus crisis of 1974, a Soviet spy satellite was launched to monitor Turkish military movements before the Russians decided, as a result of the satellite's reports, to take a low-profile approach to the explosive situation that was developing.

Evaluation of intelligence necessarily contains dangers. The evaluators may be incompetent or may misread a situation or they may colour their reports to suit their beliefs and prejudices, with potentially catastrophic consequences. President Kennedy was furious with the CIA after the Bay of Pigs fiasco; he was convinced that senior CIA officials who planned the operation simply did not appreciate the implications of what they were up to or the limited resources put at their disposal (the CIA mistakenly expected the Cuban people to rise against Fidel Castro and rally to the Bay of Pigs attacking force).

Soviet intelligence underestimated the Ghanaian opposition to Kwame Nkrumah, the late president of Ghana, who was deposed while visiting China in 1966. It cost the Russians a secure base for espionage in West Africa, as well as a lot of good will in Black Africa when the extent of their operations in Ghana was revealed after the coup. Responsibility for that failure may lie with the fact that Russian intelligence evaluators tend to be more reluctant than their counterparts in other major espionage services to volunteer detailed interpretations. They prefer, cautiously, to let their superiors in the KGB draw their own conclusions from the reports of agents, dressed up with relevant information to place those reports in an understandable setting. However, the highest ranking KGB officials do not share this reluctance to draw conclusions or press their views on the Kremlin.

Counter-espionage

According to the laws of physics, every force generates an equal and opposing force. It is the same with espionage, almost. The evolution and perfection of spying methods over the ages spawned the counter-espionage impulse. However, unlike happenings in the balanced world of physics, espionage and counter-espionage are rarely equal in extent and are not exclusively opposing forces. In fact, counter-espionage is no longer properly named. Though it still retains some of its original function detecting and neutralizing spies and clandestine enemy espionage actions-its area of activity now far transcends mere defensive operations.

At its simplest level, counter-espionage still involves security vetting of those who have access to guarded secrets and pursuit of those illegitimately trying to obtain them. In some cases, this operation can be as full of intrigue as a sophisticated spying mission, with uncovered spies often permitted to function under secret surveillance, as Penkovsky was in Moscow, strung along in the hope that they will reveal the extent of their objectives and networks. This aspect of counter-espionage is often the province of special domestic security services — the FBI in America, DI5 (formerly MI5) in Britain.

But counter-espionage has grown enormously in scope. Its primary task now is to penetrate and use adversary espionage systems. The counter-espionage agent is one of the aristocrats of the spying profession. His assignment is to discover and transmit as much as he can about an adversary intelligence organization from the best possible vantage point, from inside.

Kim Philby operated as a Russian agent for more than a decade after the Second World War while occupying successive senior positions in the British intelligence service.

Despite the fact that all major intelligence services now run recurring, intensive security spot checks on their personnel, western penetration agents are still placed in Communist espionage agencies and CIA officials are convinced that Russian secret agents operate within their organization. Modern intelligence services try to restrict possible enemy penetration with 'need to know' systems under which, no matter how senior an officer, he is permitted access only to information which he requires for his specific assignment.

However, there are dangers in this system. East German spy Guillaume was not discovered sooner by West German security because bits of information which would have immediately identified him as a possible spy were so distributed in various files that 'need to know' restrictions kept them from being readily assembled.

Agents in the field

Operational procedures for spying have become increasingly complex, structured and institutionalized over the years. The one-man operation, in which an individual embarks alone on his mission and performs it without assistance from other agents, is now exclusively the realm of spy fiction. In the real world, security has grown far too effective for the lone wolf to get very far. The agent often needs documents forged by experts. He needs assistance in transmitting his information after he has managed to acquire it. He needs help if he has to run for cover. The desired information is often sufficiently complex to require the activities of several spies operating in concert and a team of evaluators to make it meaningful. To meet the complexity of the profession, a hierarchy of function and authority has sprung up in the spy world. It is simple enough at the home base — very much like a big business set-up with chiefs, sub-chiefs and sub-sub-chiefs controlling a great number of Indians. Nor is the structure in the field overly unique.

The senior agents in the field are the station chiefs, high ranking intelligence officers occupying diplomatic posts in embassies of major countries — usually Moscow for eastern Europe; Cairo in the Middle East; London in western Europe (though Brussels is gaining in popularity). Station chiefs are the chief regional administrative espionage officers abroad, responsible for the overall functioning of espionage operations in the areas to which they are assigned. They never engage directly in missions themselves but by virtue of their background and rank, they are so well known to other intelligence services that little effort is made to conceal their identity (though publicity is unwelcome both to them and the country from which they operate through tacit reciprocal understanding. CIA London station chief Cord Meyer was publicly identified by the newspaper, *The Guardian,* soon after he took up his post as a political attaché at the American Embassy in 1973. The publicity led to consideration of his early withdrawal from London).

Despite the passing of the age of personal heroics, the key man in a spying operation remains the 'illegal' who will obtain and hand over secret information or perform other covert acts of espionage, often including dirty tricks. Although he is only one of several kinds of secret agents, he is generally what is meant when people speak of spies. He may be a national of the country he serves, trained to fit inconspicuously into the foreign adversary environment in which he will operate. More often, however, he is bought, blackmailed or recruited through other means on the spot, most likely because he already has access to the desired information, like Polish intelligence officer Josef Swiatlo, who worked for the CIA for several years before he physically defected to the United States in 1953, and like Lieutenant Colonel W. H. Whalen, arrested as a KGB spy in 1966 while working as an American army intelligence officer assigned to the Joint Chiefs of Staff.

On a level between the station chief and the 'illegal' is the *case officer,* who instructs the spy on the specifics of his mission and to whom the spy transmits acquired information or is otherwise responsible. The case officer usually, but not always, operates under diplomatic immunity. He is responsible both to his station chief and to his headquarters at home.

The Russians often establish parallel operations, deploying both diplomatically immune and 'illegal' case officers together with their respective agents — within the same areas, to guarantee regional continuity should one be uncovered. In such cases, the station chiefs control the parallel networks and keep them separated. In recent years, Russian case officers stationed in the United States have operated actively under cover of official positions they occupy at United Nations headquarters in New York as well as from the Soviet Embassy in Washington and in Russian trade missions in the United States. (Many foreign station chiefs in America prefer to be based in New York rather than Washington because of UN cover for themselves and their subordinates.) The Russians, Chinese and other Communist espionage organizations also frequently employ overseas correspondents of their national news agencies, though rarely on 'illegal' missions.

For security reasons, contact between case officer and agent is often indirect, by means of a *cut-out,* who serves exclusively as a go-between, making and maintaining contact between the two. This protects the case officer when the agent is uncovered; he can avoid detection himself and continue to control other agents on his string. Despite the risks involved, the Russians have recently sanctioned greater direct contact between case officers and agents, presumably in the hope of increasing the productive capacity of their spies. It has proved expensive for them; in little more than a decade almost 400 Soviet diplomats (many of them case officers) have been expelled for espionage activities from countries around the world.

Information and messages are passed by the spy to the cutout (or to the case officer) either through direct contact — handed over personally and secretly during ostensibly chance encounters in bars, train stations, etc. — or by use of *dead-drops.* Dead-drops are otherwise unused places where communications can be hidden to be picked up at prearranged times or after prearranged signals, like innocent sounding phone calls or newspaper advertisements. Among places commonly used as dead-drops are specified trees in forests, disused mail boxes and behind remote country milestones. Penkovsky sometimes left his messages for western agents affixed to the back of radiators in the hallways of specified Moscow apartment houses.

Safe-houses, believed free of surveillance by adversary security services, are often set up for use when prolonged and possibly recurring personal meetings between the case officer and the spy are deemed necessary. Opinions vary on whether such safe-houses are less likely to be blown in crowded city centres, suburbia or isolated rural areas. During the American Civil War, a Confederate safe-house was run by popular Washington society hostess and Confederate spy Rose Greenhow a hop, skip and a jump from the White House.

The relationship between the case officer and the spy is often complex and delicate. Unlike most case officers, the spy is in perpetual danger. His mental condition often reflects the resulting emotional turmoil. A prime duty of the case officer is to keep the spy active (unless it is advisable to have him lay low for a period) as well as useful and calm. The case officer must often fulfil the function of a confessor to a sinner, convincing the spy (particularly if he is spying against his own country) that his basic righteousness outweighs whatever transgressions he may think he is perpetrating. He must, at the same time, maintain firm control over the spy, preventing him from developing delusions of grandeur because of his contribution to his adopted cause. That could easily lead to personality conflicts between case officer and spy which could endanger the mission and everyone concerned.

The case officer must, however, make certain the spy believes his services are appreciated. Wennerstrom, only a colonel in the Swedish Air Force, was made a Soviet general to prove to him how much his services on behalf of Russia were appreciated and to keep him active. Not quite as generous when it comes to handing out rank, the Americans made Russian Colonel Penkovsky a colonel in the American army. They gilded the gift by preparing a colonel's uniform which Penkovsky delightedly tried on at a secret meeting during a visit to London while he was still an officer in Soviet military intelligence.

Intelligence services long ago came to the conclusion that a mercenary spy is, as likely as not, unreliable. A man who can be bought by one side can be bought by the other. But such is the hunger for an adversary's secret information, and such is human venality, that payment for intelligence (except to salaried personnel of intelligence agencies) is standard procedure. Method of payment varies. Some spies are on retainers, drawing fixed amounts at fixed periods either for supplying whatever information they can lay their hands on or to be on call for specific assignments. The money is paid in local currency or deposited into foreign bank accounts. Some agents are paid by productivity, but such arrangements can be troublesome. The CIA learned to its chagrin a few years ago that an agent in Hungary who was paid by piece work was remarkably productive (and, as a consequence, well paid) but that most of what he had offered was totally fabricated.

Obviously, a spy's allegiance to the cause he serves is the safest inducement. But intelligence services prefer to pay foreigners who serve them at least small sums, to bind them symbolically over and above their freely given loyalty. It's a form of insurance against a change of heart. Such sums are generally paid, for the same reason, to individuals who are blackmailed into spying.

Double agents are misnamed. By definition, they are individuals who freelance at spying, serving more than one cause, selling their services but not their allegiance. In practice, however, those known as double agents serve one cause while pretending to serve another. Spies 'turned around' by one means or another, such as the German agents who were induced to work for the British while ostensibly continuing to work for German intelligence during World War Two, fit into this category. So do Russian spies who have penetrated American intelligence, and vice versa.

Sleepers are agents planted in the bureaucracies of adversary nations to perform normal duties there, gain seniority and positions of trust, and stay clear of all possibly incriminating activity until activated as spies at propitious moments. The KGB calls them 'termites' because they bore their way into positions of influence. It requires considerable patience and the ability to fill the job taken while waiting, perhaps many years, to be brought into play as a spy. It also means playing a part in community life and often raising a family, simply as cover. Some historians are convinced that sleepers in the American State and Treasury departments were activated by the Russians as the Second World War drew to a close to provide Moscow with American diplomatic secrets which enabled the Russians to make the most of Allied conferences called to determine the political make-up of postwar Europe.

Charges were made in the British House of Lords in 1975 that sleepers had penetrated British government agencies to await the moment when they could best be of use in destroying the fabric of British society. Although some native British revolutionary groups have aspirations in that direction and may have planted such sleepers, and although other countries might wish them success, their activities are separate from that of espionage; they are the manoeuvrings of conflicting elements and forces within a country.

Why Espionage?

Though the reasons why an individual becomes a spy may often be complex, the motivations of national espionage organizations are simple and clear-cut. Espionage is an instrument for furthering national interests in a climate where confrontation between nations, even when not actual or imminent, is a possibility. What Clausewitz said about war is true for espionage as well — it is the continuation of policy by other means. It is employed to strengthen a country or neutralize an adversary's advantages.

The value of espionage in wartime is obvious. Its significance for major countries in times of peace was spelled out by CIA director William Colby, who said that for America not to undertake covert espionage operations would 'leave us with nothing between diplomatic protest and sending in the marines'.

Espionage is commonly employed by major powers to help maintain their spheres of influence. United States interest in Latin America (where there are enormous American

27

investments and which could be used as a base of operations by adversaries of the United States) has repeatedly been transformed into American espionage operations in Latin American countries. The CIA assisted elements in Chile which overthrew an elected Marxist president and installed a military dictatorship instead. It was also instrumental in overthrowing a leftist president of Guatemala and actively backs Latin American movements and personalities who can be relied upon to support American policies and objectives.

Russian determination to maintain control over East Europe and East European countries has kept the KGB active and vigilant in those countries, dominating their intelligence services and keeping an eye out for 'revisionist' tendencies. There have also been repeated attempts by the KGB to whip up a pro-Moscow coup against Yugoslavia's independent Communist leaders. Yuri Andropov, who served for many years in a liaison role between the Kremlin and its East European satellites was later to surface as director of the KGB at its Moscow headquarters.

Rich pickings for espionage agencies can often be found in countries commonly conceded to be outside the ideological and strategic struggle. Switzerland has remained a marketplace for the world of spies, with national secrets (concerning East-West rivalry, the Middle East dispute, and Russian-Chinese hostility) regularly changing hands there. The efficient Swiss security service turns a blind eye to such transactions, so long as Swiss security is not violated.

Though often futile, espionage has, at times, proved memorably effective. Worldwide German spy networks failed to save Germany from defeat in two world wars. But the Russian spy system, which flourished after the Second World War, acquired for the Russians atomic secrets they would otherwise have needed years to unravel. Cold War espionage — including spy-in-the-sky satellites — subsequently has given both America and Russia a keen awareness of each other's destructive capabilities and has, thereby, contributed significantly to the avoidance of a nuclear showdown, though such a showdown was a possibility for a generation and still is.

3.   THE ANNALS

And see the land what it is; and the people that dwelleth therein, whether they be strong or weak, few or many. And what the land is that they dwell in, whether it be good or bad; and what cities they be that they dwell in, whether in tents or strongholds.

The first recorded espionage operation in history was counter-productive. According to the Old Testament, Moses, leading the Israelites out of Egypt, dispatched spies to scout out the Promised Land. They did so and returned with word that it was indeed a land of milk and honey. They added, however, that its inhabitants were formidable and fierce. This description terrified the Israelites, whose timidity so angered God that they were made to wander the desert forty years as punishment.

Whether the report of the Israelite spies was accurate or coloured by personal aversion to combat is impossible to determine. It is certain, however, that evaluation of the report (the fear which aroused God's ire) negligently overlooked a vital factor, the prospect of divine assistance in battle.

In truth, such considerations are rare in intelligence evaluation. But another Old Testament espionage operation had a textbook simplicity to it. An agent was dispatched to determine an enemy's source of strength so that it could be neutralized — the basic objective of all major spying missions, few of which have been as successful. Knowing Samson to be the most potent force available to their Hebrew adversaries, the Philistines paid the beautiful Delilah to win his love, learn the secret of his extraordinary strength, and undermine it. It is unlikely that the success of a secret mission has ever again been signalled by a haircut, but the Old Testament account demonstrates that the significance of espionage was already well-established in biblical times.

In fact, intelligence gathering is instinctive, and not only for humans. Virtually all living creatures assess other creatures they encounter, to determine their strength and intentions, and to plot fulfilment of their own objectives. Diminutive ants dispatch scouts to study the terrain and search for food. A lion lurking in tall grass near a waterhole studies the best means of snaring a thirsty antelope; the antelope keeps an ear raised, listening for hungry lions.

Primitive cavemen undoubtedly scrutinized as best they could all strangers who appeared on the horizon. Not until the dawn of farming, the origin of stable communities, did humans begin to rely on a degree of security; not until then did they stop automatically assessing the potential menace of virtually all strangers with whom they came in contact. Nevertheless, they continued to have claims, goals and ambitions, usually related to the possession of, and craving for, territory and power. Conflict, alas, was and is a universal and central theme in human history. Intelligence gathering is one of its primary tools.

In primitive societies, soothsayers and witches provided information warriors needed for picking the time, place and occasion of battle. This information was sometimes deciphered from secrets concealed in the entrails of slaughtered chickens and other animals. Sometimes the soothsayers read omens in the stars, the winds, the clouds and the rain. In some places they still do.

But the value of more conventional espionage methods was known to the ancient world. The Chinese philosopher, Sun

Tzu, declared as long ago as the sixth century BC that 'all warfare is based on deception'. In his extraordinary primer for warriors. *The Art of War,* Sun Tzu emphasized the importance of effective espionage and counter-espionage to assure quick victory. He went so far as to categorize the types of spies to be employed, including penetration agents, double agents and expendables those planted in enemy ranks with false information (which they believe to be true) in order to be caught and to deceive enemy counter-intelligence.

Mithridates the Great (first century BC), king of Pontus in Asia Minor, was his own secret agent and an extremely able one. He ascended the throne while still a boy, almost immediately discovered that his mother was plotting to kill him, and fled. In exile, he travelled widely in surrounding lands in Asia Minor, learning the languages and ways of their peoples, as well as their military resources and the topography of their countries. Returning to Pontus as a young man, he imprisoned, then murdered his mother and various other kin, and proceeded to conquer and ravage the region he had so meticulously explored, employing the intelligence he had gathered in his boyhood explorations. (A thousand years later, King Alfred the Great, the first major English spy, is said to have disguised himself as a beggar to scout out military deployments of the invading Danes who threatened his kingdom.)

Postal censorship for counter-espionage purposes was first used by Alexander the Great as he led his army deep into Asia. Suspecting discontent among his officers, he suggested they might send personal messages home by means of official couriers he was dispatching back to Greece. He then read the letters his trusting officers had written and was able to gauge and act upon morale problems in the ranks.

Horsemen and Spymasters

No one has ever used spies more successfully for the mass conquest of land than the Mongols who swept out of northeast Asia in the thirteenth century to conquer most of the rest of Asia, the Near East, and central and eastern Europe. At first, the Mongols relied on their magnificent horsemen who ventured deep into enemy territory to reconnoitre and report back. These astounding scouts were capable of scanning enormous areas, their heads, chests and stomachs bound with bands, presumably to protect their bodies from the effects of hard riding over long distances. When foraging could not supply sustenance, they tapped the veins of their horses, drank small quantities of blood for nourishment, then sealed the wounds (it has been suggested that the vampire legends of central Europe may have had their origins with this practice).

Wherever mighty Mongol armies went, teams of outriders preceded them, charting unfamiliar terrain and military obstacles that had to be overcome. Their performance helped enable the Mongols to overwhelm armies which far outnumbered their own. As the Mongol Empire spread across the map of Eurasia, its rulers began employing other means of espionage as well. Merchants, of various nationalities, were recruited to provide information which assisted the Mongols in maintaining control over conquered territories and in spreading their conquests still further. Details were sought of rivalries between unconquered lands, to be exploited to the Mongol advantage. The greatest of the Mongol leaders, Genghis Khan, *Lord of the Earth,* was so convinced of the value of espionage that he ordered all persons caught spying against the Mongols immediately put to death.

Although Mongol espionage, intimately linked to the deployment of powerful, mobile armies, was probably the most effective spy system in history, the structure of a methodical, purposeful modern national espionage organization did not begin to emerge until the reign of the Virgin Queen in 16th-century England. Elizabeth I's spymaster, Sir Francis Walsingham, transformed the art of espionage.

Walsingham constructed an espionage edifice which, though designed to cope with specific problems of state, was to influence the development of all future espionage practice and procedure. To guard his queen and country against domestic and foreign intrigue and conspiracy, Walsingham recruited and trained a network of skilled, professional agents, some of whom he deployed abroad; he changed counter-espionage from a passive to an active component in espionage procedures; and he introduced cryptology as a standard means of espionage communications and communications interception.

All of these had been employed piecemeal and sporadically before Walsingham the practice of maintaining permanent diplomatic envoys in other states, and of using them as spies, originated in Renaissance Italy but he wove the various threads together into an enduring concept. All spymasters who followed stood on Walsingham's shoulders.

The contribution of Cardinal Richelieu (17th century) to the annals of espionage is unique in a different way. Few historical personalities have been as badly served by fiction as was Richelieu in the enchanting tale, *The Three Musketeers,* by Dumas. In that book (and subsequent films), Richelieu is pictured as a cruel man who exercised an unnatural, evil influence over the French king, whose chief minister he was, using spies and a private army exclusively to maintain his own malicious power. In fact, Richelieu's efforts, substantially assisted by the espionage apparatus manipulated by his aide, the Capuchin priest, Father Joseph, created the framework of national unity in France for the first time. They were forerunners of the exploitation of espionage for nationalistic purposes, which was later to be its major role.

In their devotion to France, the cardinal and Father Joseph subordinated their Catholic allegiance and supported Protestant forces in northern and central Europe because they feared France would otherwise be dwarfed by Catholic Austria, then the major power in Europe. The subtle intrigues of Father Joseph, which bolstered Protestant forces arrayed against Austria and which undermined Austrian authority, played a key role in depriving Austria of its European supremacy and in building France into a major entity. Domestically, the cardinal's spy network provided a continual flow of information from all corners of the country, to permit him, despite the fictional exploits of the musketeers, to neutralize decisive elements which could have obstructed the unification of the country.

With the growth of nation-states, espionage was employed increasingly as a useful, but not essential, tool. It was invoked to assist military and diplomatic initiatives which were considered basically capable of achieving their objectives, though some might not have been launched or might have failed (they often did anyway) were it not for the support of espionage operations. However, Frederick the Great of Prussia (18th century) demonstrated that espionage could serve an additional, crucial function — to compensate for potentially crippling-military shortcomings, by harnessing advantages extracted from substantial quantities of intelligence about adversary forces and intentions.

Frederick — a man of great personal intelligence, a philosopher, a poet, a gifted composer, a friend of Voltaire — personally superintended his espionage network, which directed against threats posed by the larger forces of France, Austria and Russia. He deployed a small battalion of spies —

high and middle ranking foreign personages and officials who were bribed for secrets at their disposal, others who offered snippets of information for a few coins, and Prussian secret agents infiltrated through enemy lines. Frederick himself received their reports and did his own evaluating. The results played no small part in the emergence of Prussia as a major nation and a European force, the germ from which modern Germany was to grow.

Ideological Spies and Saturation Spying

From the beginning spies had served rulers or national entities. But the American Revolution, at the end of the 18th century, produced a new concept of espionage — the ideological spy, the agent motivated by ideals. The secret agents who served George Washington's revolutionary forces were as strongly propelled to action in support of national independence and personal liberties as were the men who signed the Declaration of Independence.

Nathan Hale, the most celebrated spy of the American Revolution, was neither competent nor effective; his reputation is based exclusively on the courage with which he faced his execution after his own blunders led to his capture by the British. Some of Washington's other agents were more successful, but none were overly influential in determining the course of battle. Nevertheless, the emergence of the ideological spy opened a new era in espionage, one that was later to flourish.

Modern espionage agencies now know that virtually every scrap of information about an adversary country is potentially useful — its geography, economy, and the character of its people, as well, of course, as its political and military secrets. But, until the arrival on the scene of Wilhelm Stieber in mid-19th-century Prussia, espionage had been extremely selective. For one thing, those responsible for intelligence evaluation saw no need for vast catalogues of seemingly useless details. For another, only a limited number of agents were sent into the field or recruited there. Stieber, Bismarck's spymaster, changed all that.

He plunged into intelligence gathering with a voracious appetite for information. He wanted to know the swiftness of rivers, the penetrability of forests, the availability of food in various parts of adversary countries, the habits of military officers, everything that could possibly be learned, regardless of apparent irrelevance. He recruited the largest army of spies ever assembled, introducing a revolutionary new concept in espionage, the ordinary person as spy hotel waiters, businessmen, farmers, civil servants, store keepers, prostitutes, all required, through payment or threats, to provide information which Stieber digested and transformed into meaningful intelligence profiles of the countries against which Bismarck was to unleash his Prussian armies. Many significant factors influence the flow of history, but in the conversion of the Prussian Kingdom into the German Empire in a few short years, Stieber's role should not be underestimated. The lessons he taught intelligence agencies, which were later to develop and which were to study his methods, definitely were not.

The technological achievements of the 19th century saw the evolution of a still more penetrating dimension of espionage. The invention of the telegraph and the improvement in photographic techniques permitted spies to record and transmit their stolen secrets and other intelligence information in ways never possible before. During the First World War, aerial reconnaissance made its debut as a significant intelligence gathering instrument, heralding an age of mechanized spying which was to carry espionage practices into outer space.

But, despite technological innovations, the human

component, the secret agent, remained active. The Second World War saw the re-emergence of the ideological spy, the individual moved to serve an espionage organization because of his beliefs. Many agents in Europe were recruited by the Allies because of their hatred of fascism. Some were drawn to the German cause because of sympathy with fascism. During and after the war, Russia was hugely successful in building productive spy networks based on non-Russian agents who were Communists or Communist sympathizers, while the United States and other western countries were successful, though less so, in recruiting agents in Communist countries who were motivated by a hatred of Communism.

The technological impact on espionage procedures and practices — particularly the use of orbiting satellites and electronic devices — has been the most recent primary development in the world of spying. But, organizationally, the major new innovation has been the emergence of national espionage agencies as influential and complex instruments of power and activity; primarily the KGB and the CIA, but also the bureaux of other countries for whose basic policy objectives spies have been widely deployed — China seeking to become a superpower; South Africa seeking to prop up its vulnerable race theories of government and society; a number of Latin American countries seeking to short-circuit coups-in-the-making in havens abroad.

The fact that espionage agencies sometimes serve also to persecute and stifle domestic dissidents diminishes whatever glamour normally attaches itself to spy work. But the espionage agencies are, nevertheless, the logical outgrowth of all that has transpired in man's search for knowledge, and for the power he has long believed would flow from it.

4.   THE AMERICANS

I am trying to run a secret intelligence service,' William Colby despairingly informed congressional inquisitors in Washington in June, 1975. But, through circumstances largely beyond his control, Colby, the then newly appointed director of America's Central Intelligence Agency, was having a lot of trouble succeeding in his objective.

CIA secrets were being splashed across the front pages of newspapers around the world. CIA practices and procedures were being exposed to public scrutiny. CIA officials were being interrogated in depth by congressional committees. The agency, the baby among national espionage services, had offended against American law and congressional restrictions and was paying a heavy price for its transgressions.

Never before had an espionage agency been so thoroughly in disgrace and publicly belittled as was the CIA. The agony of its officials was diminished only by the fact that they were being cut down to size by fellow Americans rather than adversaries.

Some of the CIA's excesses had been pinpointed by a committee of conservative Americans set up by President Gerald Ford and headed by Vice President Nelson Rockefeller. The congressional investigations probed even deeper into CIA derelictions, only to be surpassed by still more incriminating reports and allegations in some American newspapers. It was demonstrated that, contrary to its charter which confines the agency to foreign activities, the CIA had engaged in widespread domestic security operations.

It had, for example, methodically spied on domestic dissident organizations. It had compiled dossiers on thousands of Americans. It had intercepted and read mail passing through the American postal system, provoking a humiliating public rebuke from the American postmaster-general, an order barring the CIA from access to 'any kind of mail in the custody of the postal service'.

The agency had experimented with the hallucinatory drug LSD on unsuspecting Americans, including a civilian employee of the Department of the Army who shortly afterwards leapt to his death from a tenth-storey hotel window. While security screening a number of American citizens employed by the agency itself, it had broken into and searched their homes without search warrants required by law.

There were also more serious, unsubstantiated charges — that the CIA had been implicated in the assassination of President John Kennedy and, without authorization, had planted operatives in the White House. By the time the disclosures of its illegal domestic operations gathered momentum, virtually any charge of improper activity could be made against the agency and seem not to be beyond the realm of possibility. Testimony from a man with proven Mafia connections that he had been recruited by the CIA to assassinate Cuban leader Castro and that the agency had been implicated in plots against other foreign leaders corroborated the impression that it had gone wildly astray in interpreting its authority and assignment.

It was clear that, although a mere three decades old (the British and Russian intelligence services have had centuries of experience on which to draw), the CIA had not been noticeably restrained as it groped its way towards maturity. It had plunged forcefully, and often recklessly, into an ambitious programme of protecting and promoting American national interests. If some of the procedures it employed have been justifiably condemned as intolerable by American standards, it should be pointed out that many of them are part and parcel of the operational practice of some other national intelligence services, few of which are answerable to so vigilant a press and legislature as those in America.

A catalogue of CIA operations in recent years reveals the impact which a major national espionage organization can have on international affairs. The agency was instrumental in bringing down at least two governments which threatened American interests (in Iran and Guatemala) and in preparing the way for the restoration of governments in those two countries more sympathetic to American policies. It ran an open war (in Laos) and a major guerrilla campaign (in Vietnam), both of which were ultimately unsuccessful. It helped suppress a guerrilla insurrection (in the Philippines) and botched what was meant to be a popular uprising (in Cuba). It helped the late Egyptian leader, Gamal Abdul Nasser, climb to power and then tried to undermine his authority when Nasser's policies began to conflict with those of the United States.

It was accused of conspiring in the murder of a left-wing president of the Belgian Congo (now Zaire) and a right-wing dictator in the Dominican Republic. It established contact with disgruntled intelligence officials in Communist countries, thereby promoting an influx of well-informed defectors to the West who assisted western intelligence services in combatting KGB activities. It established a network of agents around the world and can claim credit for many American successes in the Cold War confrontation with Russia, as well as responsibility for many of its failures.

Background

Until the Second World War, espionage played an

exceedingly minor role in American strategic thinking. George Washington, commanding America's revolutionary army, knew the value of intelligence and fielded as many spies as his limited budget and manpower resources permitted. A corps of agents, under Washington's spymaster, Major Benjamin Tallmadge of Connecticut, was organized to penetrate British lines. Dedicated revolutionaries all, the agents were highly motivated and particularly effective in monitoring the loose talk of British officers in the popular coffee-houses of occupied New York. But America's first experience with espionage proved to have little influence on the course of actual combat. Not until the Civil War, almost a century later, did spies again appear in any significant number upon the stage of American history.

The War Between the States inevitably found many Confederate sympathizers in Union territory and vice versa, with the result that both sides were flooded with information which self-appointed agents considered useful to their respective causes. Some of it was; most of it was not. Both North and South also deployed officially commissioned spies to penetrate each other's lines. But, though President Abraham Lincoln sanctioned the appointment of Scottish-born Allan Pinkerton (who was later to establish the world's first major private detective agency) to set up a secret service to operate against the Confederacy, it was considered only a temporary expedient and was permitted to wither away after the war.

The attitude of American military commanders tended to militate against the establishment of an enduring American espionage service. Most of them considered the gathering of intelligence through devious means (except by military scouts) and other espionage operations to be unworthy of soldiers. At the start of the First World War, only a handful of War Department personnel were assigned to gathering intelligence.

In view of the influence they wielded and the resources put at their disposal, they might just as well have been on Mars.

However, America's first involvement in a major international conflagration in 1917 soon made it evident that it was frivolous and unwise to neglect intelligence gathering. German secret agents had almost succeeded in embroiling the United States in a war with Mexico to divert its energies from the struggle in Europe. Successes registered by British intelligence, particularly in cracking German codes, demonstrated the importance of setting up an espionage agency. With British and French guidance, an American military intelligence division, G-2, established earlier but never more than a facade, was beefed-up, introduced to the mysteries of international espionage, and put to work.

But the usefulness of an active intelligence service continued to elude most American leaders and G-2 soon bogged down in military bureaucracy, except for a highly efficient cryptography bureau which survived the war. It continued to function, intercepting and deciphering foreign diplomatic communications, until 1929 when its activities were brought to the attention of the puritanical Secretary of State, Henry Stimson. Stimson was appalled. He muttered angrily, 'Gentlemen do not read each other's mail' and had it disbanded.

As a consequence, when it became apparent that World War Two was inevitable, and that America would be drawn in, the country again found itself without even the semblance of an espionage service. General Dwight Eisenhower (soon to be Allied commander in Europe and later president of the United States) and other American military leaders were horrified when they belatedly became aware of the significance of this shortcoming.

New York lawyer William Donovan, a decorated First

43

World War officer, was summoned by President Franklin
Roosevelt and instructed to explore the situation. As a result of
'Wild Bill' Donovan's report, the American Central Office of
Information was set up to deal both with propaganda and
espionage. This arrangement proved cumbersome and the
Office of Strategic Services (OSS) was created under Donovan
to deal exclusively with espionage.

The OSS put in a respectable showing during the war,
penetrating enemy lines for intelligence gathering and
sabotage missions and establishing contact with and assisting
resistance forces in enemy occupied territory. It was also
America's first real experience in recruiting foreign agents to
operate in foreign countries, a practice that would be much
expanded when the CIA was later formed.

Despite dramatic feats in the field by OSS operatives, the
organization's major achievements were those of its Research
and Analysis division, a battery of brains which collated and
interpreted agents' reports, enemy radio communications, and
information from enemy media, much of it acquired in neutral
countries. By the time the war ended, the OSS had a staff of
more than ten thousand and a budget to match. America had
entered the business of international espionage.

Catalyst in Canada

The American government was uncertain what to do with
its new espionage capabilities. Those who had a personal
interest in maintaining a central intelligence bureau said there
was a continuing need for such an organization. Others agreed
for reasons of operational efficiency. But chiefs of military
services, who now had active intelligence divisions of their
own, insisted that the work, where needed, could safely be left
to them. Others felt that while spying on other nations had
served its purpose in wartime, it was basically inconsistent
with American traditions and values, exorbitantly expensive,

and should be abandoned. The Cold War and Igor Gouzenko helped resolve the dispute.

The Gouzenko escapade took place in Canada, close enough to the United States in geography and political philosophy for its impact to be felt there as much as in Canada itself. In September, 1945, a mere month after the end of World War Two, Gouzenko, a young cipher clerk at the Russian Embassy in Ottawa, defected, taking with him enough secret documents to prove that the Russians had been busily constructing aggressive spy networks in countries with which they had just been allied in mortal combat. The Gouzenko revelations showed that the Russians had two major goals, one immediate, one long-term: (1) stealing western atom secrets; (2) subverting non-Communist governments through the infiltration of Communist agents.

The Gouzenko disclosures were to lead, over a period of years, to the paranoiac McCarthyite era in America during which the search for subversives was transformed into an unreasonable and frequently irrational witchhunt. However, the disclosures also led to the arrest of Russian atom spies in Britain, Canada and the United States. Most significantly, the proof of Russian espionage activity (together with other unavoidable signs that the Cold War was shaping up; overwhelmed residual doubts that the United States needed an effective central espionage agency of its own to meet the Soviet challenge.

The OSS had been disbanded when the war ended; many of its key personnel had been distributed among various intelligence units in the State and War Departments. Now steps were taken to bring them together again in a unified intelligence agency. The CIA, responsible to the National Security Council (made up of the president, vice president, and secretaries of State and Defence), was established by an act of congress in 1947.

Its purpose was to coordinate, correlate and evaluate intelligence gathered by the various government and military intelligence units already functioning. But it was also authorized to 'perform such other functions and duties related to intelligence as the National Security Council may direct'. The organization soon became known around the world for those 'other functions and duties', a phrase increasingly treated by the CIA as authorization to do as it saw fit.

Judging from achievement, the organization's performance during its early years was meager. The primary adversary was Russian imperialistic Communism, but CIA agents dispatched to Eastern Europe (and those recruited there) could do little more than report on how their rivals in the KGB, backed up by the intimidating presence of the Russian army, were helping create the conditions which led to Communist seizures of power in Poland, Czechoslovakia, Bulgaria, Romania and Hungary. Aware of their inexperience, American intelligence chiefs gratefully accepted the assistance of the British in planning their organizational structure and many of their early operations. Among those who helped was Russian spy Kim Philby, who was highly placed in British intelligence and who kept the Russians informed on a wide range of CIA activities, with frequently catastrophic consequences for the agency (see chapter on *The Spy Above Suspicion).* One American official said the CIA would have been better off staying altogether clear of covert espionage operations during the period when friend Philby was helping out.

But not all the mistakes perpetrated by the CIA during its toddler years can be blamed on *force majeure* or treachery. Many of its errors were the product of sheer inexperience, compounded by an exaggerated sense of power nourished by a massive secret budget. The agency squandered money recruiting armies of spies around the world, many of whom fabricated reports to appear to be earning their keep, and some of whom were agents of the KGB or other espionage services.

It developed an obsession for secrecy for secrecy, veiling in mystery certain aspects of CIA work (research and analysis, for example) which, if kept less in the shadows without revealing classified information, might have softened the clock-and-dagger image the organization developed around the world.

Ironically, in some of its successful operations, greater secrecy would have been advisable. The CIA's participation in the overthrow of the leftist regimes of Mohammed Mossadegh in oil-rich Iran in 1953 and Jacobo Arbenz in Guatemala in 1954 could have been much less obvious. In fact, despite the ostentatious veil of secrecy, CIA methods were sometimes so ham-fisted that the Russians — hardly light-fingered in performance themselves — and others were able to blame economic disaster in poorer countries and even natural calamities, like droughts, on CIA gimmicks, and a lot of people believed them. Though such gimmicks, rarely expedient, were not commonly found in the CIA's bag of tricks, there were moments when unsavoury resourcefulness got the better of judicious restraint. President Kennedy was furious when he learned that the agency had doctored a shipment of Russian-bound Cuban sugar to make it unpalatable — the intention had been to undermine the Cuban economy and bring down its anti-American leaders.

But despite mistakes and embarrassments, or perhaps because of them, the early years were a period of intensive learning for the CIA. It gradually grew aware of what it should and should not attempt and what it could and could not accomplish. It learned that sheer extravagance in financing operations did not guarantee success. It learned that sprawling networks of spies feeding in masses of marginally useful bits of information were not nearly as valuable as a few effective secret agents operating under deep cover in the field like the source of Premier Khrushchev's devastating speech outlining the enormity of Stalin's crimes against the Russian people, which the CIA disseminated to the world and which the Russians have themselves never made public. It learned the importance of establishing and maintaining contact with potentially friendly-revolutionary forces, particularly in Africa, instead of reflexively relying on formerly reliable but now tottering regimes.

After financing remnants of the Nationalist Chinese force which had fled to Burma (and began operating a lucrative opium trade there), the CIA learned it was a waste of effort and sometimes of good men to try to overthrow Communism in China. It learned that it was wiser to fuel the feud between China and Russia by subtle means rather than through exposable operations which might backfire. Most important, it learned that America's enormous reservoir of technological ability could be harnessed to transform espionage into 'a new ballgame'.

In the mid-1950s, the CIA developed the high-flying U-2 spy plane. The first U-2 overflight of the Soviet Union, identifying and pinpointing military and industrial installations, put the spy networks the Americans had cultivated on the ground in Russia to shame. Even more impressive reconnaissance aircraft were developed, with still more sophisticated photographic capabilities. They were, in turn, outpaced by spy satellites girdling the globe, the achievements of which were beyond CIA interpretive capacities and which, therefore, came under the jurisdiction of another branch of the American intelligence conglomerate.

The use of 'illegals' in Russia gradually became more

selective. They were, however, still deployed to gather political, military, scientific and economic intelligence beyond the reach of CIA officers stationed at the American embassy in Moscow and other European Communist capitals, and to try to answer questions which spy craft cameras raised to fill in details and explain away riddles.

The CIA research and evaluation efforts attracted much acclaim and respect within American government circles and the CIA itself began accumulating the aura of awe and reverence across America which 'good guys' acquire in cops-and-robbers films. But it was to be short-lived. The agency's massive mishandling of the 1961 Bay of Pigs invasion of Cuba left it vulnerable and exposed to criticism and administrative attack.

It had confidently assumed that when CIA-trained Cuban exiles landed on the beach, a popular uprising against Fidel Castro would erupt and that America's only adversary in Latin America would be overthrown. The entire operation was a fiasco, planned in cloak-and-dagger fashion by an autonomous CIA unit, without the full benefit of the agency's research and analysis facilities. It was planned on the mistaken assumption that Castro was essentially unpopular and that the Cuban people were aching for an opportunity to rise against him. It was planned also with the groundless assumption that American planes would go into action, if needed, to support the exiles on the landing beach. But President Kennedy, who had not been consulted about that aspect of an operation he had been assured was a sure thing, angrily refused to commit the planes, thus eliminating whatever prospect there had been that at least the landing might succeed, permitting the invaders to take to the Cuban hills as guerrillas, as Castro himself had once done.

Backlash

The Bay of Pigs operation was so amateurish that Kennedy, a firm believer in the importance of an effective intelligence agency, was pressed by some of his aides to dismantle the CIA altogether, and considered doing so. The agency had seriously embarrassed the United States, as well as Kennedy personally, who was held responsible around the world for aggression against a small nation. He was also blamed by many for the death and imprisonment of the CIA-trained invaders, virtually all of whom were anti-Communist Cuban refugees, cut down or captured on the beach because the promised air cover did not materialize. Later it would be alleged, without substantiation, that vengeful anti-Communist Cubans were involved in the assassination of Kennedy.

Instead of disbanding the CIA, Kennedy had several top agency officials put out to pasture and ordered a thorough review of American intelligence operations. The CIA could not escape unscathed. Since its inception, it had been officially responsible to the National Security Council, but generally had done as it liked. After the Bay of Pigs, a National Security Council committee (most recently called the '40 Committee' after the number of a directive concerning its functions) began exercising much firmer control over CIA foreign operations.

Proposed CIA operations were subjected to greater preliminary analysis of objectives, methods and prospects. Some observers attribute the comparative discretion with which the CIA handled its substantial involvement in Congolese turmoil in the early 1960s, when pro-Communist forces were defeated by pro-western Congolese elements, to the restraining hand clamped on the agency's shoulder.

However, the fighting in Southeast Asia in the 1960s placed a new strain on the organization. An international agreement that Laos should remain neutral and independent proved stillborn. Fearing Communist encroachment in Asia, heralded by North Vietnam's bid to gain supremacy throughout Indochina, the National Security Council authorized the CIA to mount a major operation in Laos. It moved in with enough funds and weapons to field an army of almost 40,000 Meo tribesmen, reinforced by thousands of CIA-financed Thai mercenaries, and backed by CIA pilots giving support in CIA planes, flying from CIA-manned airfields. To ferry in supplies, the agency made use of one of the seemingly private airlines it had established to cope with the problem of transport, for men and equipment, when secrecy was desired and when suspicions might be aroused by using military facilities. To maintain their cover, these CIA airlines operated on a commercial basis as well, sometimes making embarrassingly large profits. (Set up to cover secret operations, these so-called proprietary companies — which included engineering firms, security consultancies, various contracting outfits and other companies as well as airlines — gradually became a multi-million dollar chain of enterprises which, to the CIA's ever-growing chagrin, competed successfully with private American companies; another reason for keeping their true identity confidential.)

The agency became increasingly implicated in Southeast Asia when American involvement in the Vietnam War grew to massive proportions. Among the tasks the CIA took on was a series of guerrilla campaigns against the Communist Vietcong, employing specially trained Republic of Vietnam cadre and utilizing terror tactics similar to those employed by the Vietcong, including torture and assassination. Its *Operation Phoenix* was designed to rip apart the Vietcong's clandestine command structure in South Vietnam. The CIA indicated that more than 20,000 Vietcong were killed before the operation ended. Other reports put the figure much higher.

Whatever the success or failure of CIA activity in southeast Asia, it became apparent that the agency was being called upon to perform functions which defied and distorted the traditional concept of espionage which was, supposedly, its only reason for existence. It was devoting much of its energies and committing many of its best men to what was, in fact, soldier work. In addition, it was becoming caught up in the bitter debate about the rights and wrongs of the Vietnam War which divided the American people. Most damaging of all, its top officials grew so determined to paint an optimistic picture of the American military position in Vietnam that they committed the most serious error of which intelligence personnel are capable; they began believing only what they wanted to believe. They rejected and, what was worse, they buried reports from their own trained analysts about serious distortions in the military assessment of the situation, thereby contributing to the extent of the American defeat. At one point, the agency suppressed a correct report which it had itself commissioned and which estimated Vietcong troop strength in South Vietnam at *more than twice* the estimate officially used by the Pentagon in planning anti-Vietcong strategy. In classical espionage terms, this was an offence far exceeding the agency's domestic transgressions. To do its job properly, an intelligence service must be true to itself.

Ideological Combat

In its early, uncomplicated days, before the CIA had been exposed to the blinding light of publicity and public criticism, it took upon itself the task of combating the ideological influence of Communism and anti-American propaganda. It sought to influence world opinion through clandestine support for organizations and publications which it believed could effectively do the job on its behalf. Among them were such intellectual journals as the British *Encounter* magazine, the American National Student Association, and trade unions and research groups in many parts of the non-Communist world. The object was not to control those groups, which could have been counter-productive, but to help them continue performing in their own way, which tended to undermine the inroads of Communist ideology.

When this bankrolling operation was exposed, at first by a radical American magazine in 1967, the CIA and embarrassed recipient organizations (most of which genuinely had not known the source of their 'laundered' subsidies) were widely condemned as having served American imperial objectives. Some of the recipients (including publications which would have gone bankrupt but for the CIA subsidies) made only token noises of outraged innocence. But, badly bitten by the adverse publicity, the agency served notice that it was getting out of the 'rich uncle' business.

Nevertheless, use of funds to prop up needy, potentially influential outfits whose interests coincided with those of the United States was considered justified by CIA officials, particularly when adversary espionage agencies were underwriting adversary groups and publications. Lavish expenditure of CIA funds on such causes was toned down and rationalized but the subsidies continued. Selected useful foreign political, cultural and economic organizations and media went on receiving discreet contributions.

American funds were supplied to try to influence elections in Italy where a Communist take-over was possible — and still is. CIA subsidies were even more widely distributed in Latin America. Disclosures in 1974 that the CIA contributed substantial sums to help those in Chile who ultimately overthrew Marxist president, Salvador Allende, unleashed further disclosures. It also unleashed intensified criticism from those in America who charged that the CIA was unduly involved in the foreign affairs of other countries, including some which posed no threat to American interests.

Publicity, naming names and places, had serious consequences for the CIA. The morale of its operatives and officials was shattered. Their foreign agents and allies, convinced that their own activities might feature in the next morning's headlines, became increasingly unwilling to cooperate. Many CIA foreign sources dried up completely. At a time when a determined Communist effort was being made to split Portugal off from its western allies, when the entire southern flank of the North Atlantic alliance was threatened with political collapse and a Russian naval build-up, and when rival pro-western and pro-Russian elements were contending for dominance in Africa and the Middle East, the CIA was virtually incapacitated.

CIA intelligence reports to American policy-making organs became sparse and insufficiently informative. Defence Secretary James Schlesinger complained that CIA sources of information had been 'dramatically reduced'. President Ford called the contraction of CIA services 'tragic'. Traditional American suspicion of clandestine governmental activity had reared again with a vengeance.

However, in contrast to previous attitudes, there was now general acceptance in America of the ultimate need for an effective intelligence agency. Even the CIA's harshest domestic critics conceded that a research and analysis division to monitor international areas of American interest was necessary. Others continued to maintain that an American espionage agency had to be empowered to employ resources and methods similar to those of America's adversaries, no matter how unpalatable this might be to those anxious about unsavoury clandestine activities. Though attitudes had changed, America was still left seeking a proper role for its intelligence services to play. Though the organizational framework of those services remained intact to meet essential and emergency requirements, it's likely to be some time before that role is clearly defined and accepted again.

America's Intelligence Establishment

An anonymous complex of buildings at Langley, Virginia, a few miles from Washington, is CIA headquarters. Officially, the CIA has a staff of about 16,000, but it employs thousands of others as well, on contract or temporary basis, many of them through the auspices of its proprietary companies. No doubt, the pressure to which the agency has recently been subjected will result in many changes, with the likelihood that its personnel roles will be reduced.

The director of the CIA, appointed by the President, is responsible to the National Security Council and, ultimately to the President. He and his deputy director concern themselves mostly with high policy matters and liaison with government officials and congress. They usually have little to do with the day-to-day operations of the agency.

The CIA has four main directorates: operations (which deals with espionage and counter-espionage and includes divisions dealing with specific geographic areas of the world); intelligence (which deals with research and evaluation); science and technology (which deals with scientific intelligence procedures and 'special projects'); and administration (which deals with logistics and CIA security). The chiefs of these directorates are key members of the CIA Management Committee which includes the CIA comptroller and certain other logistics officers.

Proposals for operations can originate anywhere along the chain of command for consideration by a directorate chief, the Management Committee, the deputy director, the director or the National Security Council itself, depending on the scope or possible consequences of the proposed action. In practice, the 'need to know' secrecy restrictions, nurtured by fear of possible KGB infiltration, have meant that key sections of the agency were often kept in the dark on various operations. CIA officials are concerned that a backlash against 'need to know' precautions might damage the agency's internal security.

Although the CIA has primary responsibility for United States intelligence services, and although its director is also Director of Central Intelligence for the American government, the CIA is only part of America's intelligence community which, all told, employs an estimated 200,000 persons and is budgeted at over six billion dollars.

A separate bureau, the National Security Agency, with a bigger staff and a heftier budget than the CIA, devotes its considerable energies to intercepting and deciphering foreign communications around the world. It is a herculean assignment for which the NSA is equipped with an astounding array of electronic equipment, deployed in key places in various corners of the globe. Domestic upheaval and international squabbles affecting Ethiopia, Turkey, Cyprus and a number of other countries have recently compelled the NSA to contract and reorient its network of monitoring posts.

In addition to the CIA and the NSA, the three military services retain active intelligence-gathering units. (A special Air Force section runs the spy-in-the-sky satellite operation.) The State Department's intelligence service learned of border clashes between China and Russia in the 1960s long before they became public knowledge. The Atomic Energy Commission, Treasury Department and Drug Enforcement Agency also have intelligence bureaux of their own. Unlike the CIA, these bureaux are buried deep within their parent organizations and are, thereby, generally concealed from public attention.

The Foreign Intelligence Advisory Board, with

representatives of the various branches of America's intelligence community, holds regular meetings to coordinate their efforts.

Inevitably, however, there is overlapping and rivalry, particularly between the Pentagon and the CIA. There is also considerable duplication of headquarters functions, personnel and expenditure, which is likely to come under close scrutiny as a result of the crisis of confidence in the CIA.

5.   THE RUSSIANS

In September, 1971, the British government ordered 105 Russian diplomats and trade officials to leave the country. It was an extraordinary step, the largest single expulsion ever of accredited diplomats by any country in peacetime. It was also a stinging rebuke to the Russians. Had they retaliated for this humiliation by severing diplomatic relations with Britain, it would not have been a complete surprise. Moscow made do, however, with a comparatively mild protest to the British government and let the storm blow itself out.

The expelled men were all spies, agents of the KGB. Their activities in Britain were described by the British Foreign Office as 'inadmissible'. Their primary objective, in effect the objective of most of the Russian diplomatic contingent in London at the time, was to acquire, illegally (and sometimes through crude blackmail and bribery), British military and industrial secrets.

Though their ousting from Britain was a setback for the KGB, it had long before come to the conclusion that, in the give-and-take of espionage, you win a few and you lose a few, and that it is best not to make too much of either. Too great an outcry from Moscow would have attracted even greater attention to the fact that most Soviet diplomats abroad are active KGB agents whose diplomatic duties serve only to legitimize their presence in countries they spy on. The added publicity would have focused increased interest on Soviet espionage activity, which has ranged from blackmail to murder and covered a lot of ground in between.

The KGB is, in fact, far more than a national espionage agency. As an administrative and operational edifice, it is massive in dimension and unique in history. Not only does it function to further Soviet national interests through an unrivalled number of espionage and counter-espionage agents and operations around the world, but it is the instrument through which Soviet leaders police their own country. It is the tool with which they suppress all threats to their control of political, economic and social developments within the Soviet Union. Among those threats, real or imagined, are outcroppings of national feelings among the many national groupings in the Soviet Union (Ukrainians, Latvians, Tartars, etc.), criticism of Soviet leaders or their policies, religious movements, and literary, artistic and educational non-conformity.

Beginnings

Russia has been cursed with an oppressive secret police for virtually all of its recorded history. The tradition may have been inherited from the Mongols who were masters of Russia for more than two centuries and who maintained thorough surveillance and ruthless control of the peoples of all the lands they conquered. The czars, who ruled Russia after the Mongol tide withdrew, tried to establish the same omniscient authority. Ivan the Terrible, Peter the Great and Catherine the Great were among the Russian rulers who paid particular attention to the maintenance of active intelligence services whose primary function was to uncover and undermine plots by those in the Russian aristocracy who hoped to seize power.

When egalitarian ideas, engendered by the French Revolution, spread eastward to Russia and secret societies, dedicated to democratic principles, sprang up, Czar Nicholas I restructured the existing secret police apparatus to make it more effective in coping with such new and dangerous ideas.

The assassination of his successor, Czar Alexander II (1881) led to the foundation of the *Ochrana,* the most feared and repressive political police the modern world had, until then, known.

Paranoia was the *Ochrana's* propelling impulse. Every Russian who, it was thought, might conceivably be critical of the Czar, for personal or political reasons, was watched and his movements were recorded. *Ochrana* agents were planted in underground opposition groups and, posing as activists, frequently provoked or even performed seditious acts (including the assassination of officials) which seemed to justify the *Ochrana's* legal terror in the name of law and order. Though all records were destroyed later, it is believed that, before becoming a genuine revolutionary, Joseph Stalin had been an *Ochrana* agent.

The *Ochrana* was feared and hated by Russian revolutionaries and one of the first acts of the Bolsheviks, when they seized power in 1917 was to obliterate the organization. Within a month, however, the Bolsheviks established a secret police of their own, an agency that was to become more effective, more merciless and more important historically than the *Ochrana* had ever been. The *Cheka* (the initials stand for the All-Russian Extraordinary Commission for Combating Counter-Revolution and Sabotage) was hastily created to fill the gap left when the czarist secret police was eliminated.

Lenin, the Bolshevik leader, realized how precarious his revolution was. Rival revolutionary groups hatched plots against the fledgling Soviet government. Anti-Bolshevik forces were gathering to attempt a counter-revolution. The First World War, in which Russia had been a major participant, was still in progress and Russia's former allies were soon to transform their bitterness at Russia's withdrawal from the battlefield and their fear of Communism into military intervention designed to overthrow the Bolsheviks. Russia was hungry and in turmoil.

Lenin was convinced that the establishment of a potent secret police organization was necessary and urgent if the Bolsheviks, who constituted a comparatively small political clique, were to retain power. Feliks Edmundovich Dzerzhinsky, a Polish Bolshevik of aristocratic origins, was assigned the task of building and directing the *Cheka.* Dzerzhinsky was authorized to seize, imprison and execute anyone his new organization considered a possible danger to the Bolsheviks. He bluntly explained his mission — 'We stand for organized terror'. And Lenin unhesitatingly sanctioned his methods.

Communist Terror

The *Cheka* campaign of terror was monumental. The stunted roots of the Mongol secret police, of Ivan the Terrible's *Oprichniki,* and of the *Ochrana* sprouted anew, and flourished. Conspiracies, more often than not imagined, fabricated or provoked by *Cheka* agents, were exposed and smashed. Individuals were shot at the mere suggestion that they might be involved in counter-revolutionary activity, a very loosely interpreted concept. Tens of thousands were executed. An atmosphere of pathological suspicion and profound fear settled like a shroud over the Soviet Union.

The *Cheka* was succeeded by the GPU (State Political Directorate) in 1922. It became OGPU (Unified State Political Directorate) the following year, and later took other names in the constant rearrangements (often purposeless) to which bureaucratic governments so often seem addicted. Whatever its name, its objective remained the same — the maintenance of an atmosphere of terror to sustain Communist rule. Behind the formidable structures of their successive secret police agencies, Communist leaders were able to retain power under circumstances which would have shattered a dozen successive democratic governments — the chaos left by the revolution, a devastating famine, the imprisonment of millions of persons in labour camps, the disaster of the Second World War (for which Russian leaders left their country wretchedly unprepared and which claimed an estimated twenty million Russian lives), and Russia becoming a military superpower while its people lagged well behind westerners in standard of living.

During the early years of the Communist regime, the Soviet state security apparatus largely confined its attentions to domestic matters. But by the time the KGB was created in 1954 to inherit responsibility for state security, Russian espionage agents had long been active in foreign countries.

During the 1920s, Soviet agents, operating under the auspices of the Comintern (the Russian-dominated Communist International) attempted but failed to promote Communist revolutions in western and central Europe. Their efforts were often crude and obvious in terms of modern-day espionage methods. They frequently jeopardized efforts of the Soviet government to gain diplomatic recognition from other countries, as in the case of a Soviet offer of financial assistance to British miners during the 1926 British general strike.

But generally, Stalin, who had succeeded Lenin as Russian leader in 1924, was preoccupied with domestic agricultural failures, industrial backwardness and Russia's general economic tribulations, as well as the maintenance of his reign of terror at home. He had little time or energy to spare for foreign adventures, except for occasional pet projects, such as the assassination in western Europe of disciples of his hated adversary, the former Bolshevik military chief Leon Trotsky, and later of Trotsky himself in Mexico in 1940.

Despite the fact that, from the beginning, the Soviet intelligence apparatus played a central role in Russian affairs, its successive directors proved remarkably vulnerable to internal upheaval within the Soviet hierarchy and to premature demise. Genrik Yagoda (director, 1934-1936) incurred Stalin's displeasure, was denounced as a czarist spy and a thief, and was executed, along with hundreds of his top officers during the great Soviet purges of the 1930s. Yagoda's successor, Nikolai Yezhov (1936-1938) who also played no small part in organizing those purges, succumbed to them as well. He was dismissed amidst accusations of anti-Soviet activity and disappeared without a trace. Lavrenti Beria (1938-1953), who was feared by his colleagues and who plotted to seize control of Russia after Stalin's death, acted too slowly and was executed by those who grasped the leadership of the country before he could.

The Second World War

When the growth of Nazi power in Germany heralded the Second World War and, more specifically, the war between Germany and Russia, Soviet security officials again began emphasizing foreign operations. The GRU (Soviet military intelligence), concerned as it was with strategic problems, had already been busily functioning in that area. Now local Communist organizations in Germany and elsewhere in Western Europe were put at the disposal of Soviet secret agents, many of whom were natives of the countries to which they were dispatched to serve Soviet interests. Government agencies and other official bodies were infiltrated to acquire information useful to Moscow and to try to influence the policies of their countries. 'Sleepers' were put into the field, often businessmen, civil servants and professional people, to await the moment when they could be of optimum use. That moment came when Germany — breaking the German-Soviet Friendship Pact which Stalin had agreed to sign two years earlier — invaded Russia in 1941.

Western Communist parties, which had been condemning the Allied line-up against Germany, were transformed overnight into energetic anti-German movements. But, of greater significance was the activity of Russian spies, many of them planted in strategic positions.

Throughout the Second World War, Soviet agents fed Moscow a steady flow of important strategic and diplomatic information. Richard Sorge, in Tokyo, was able to tell his Soviet superiors that the Japanese did not intend to attack the Soviet Union and thereby permitted them to make crucial strategic changes. The information sent back by Leopold Trepper, head of the 'Red Orchestra' Soviet spy network in Western Europe was later said by a German general to have cost the Germans hundreds of thousands of troops. The 'Lucy Ring', operating out of Switzerland, radioed Moscow daily reports on planned German troop movements on the Eastern Front, obtained (possibly with the help of British intelligence) from within the German Army high command. Had the Russians been better prepared in the early part of the war, the information provided by their secret agents would have saved them much of the destruction and savagery inflicted on their country by the Nazi invaders. As it was, the spy reports made the Russian position less hopeless than it was originally and contributed significantly to Russian successes as the war progressed.

Postwar Developments

The huge losses and enormous devastation Russia suffered during the war reinforced its traditional xenophobia and suspicion. After the war, the Soviet espionage services were reorganized to place still greater emphasis on operations against other countries, particularly against the United States whose sole possession of the atomic bomb was considered by Moscow an intolerable menace. In their quest for atomic secrets, the Russians employed a great number of 'illegals', including the British scientist Allan Nunn May and the German-born refugee scientist Klaus Fuchs, both of whom worked on nuclear fission, and a long list of couriers and intermediaries, the best known of whom were the Americans, Julius and Ethel Rosenberg, who were caught, tried and executed in the United States.

Russian success in the pursuit of atomic secrets stimulated a new aggressiveness in Soviet overseas espionage procedures. The possibility of diplomatic embarrassment or even serious international incident did not seem to worry Moscow overly. In 1960, the respected West German parliamentarian Alfred Frenzel, a member of the important *Bundestag* defence committee, was exposed as a KGB spy of long standing. Frenzel's espionage contacts had been with the Czechoslovak intelligence service. The KGB often used the espionage apparatuses of Russia's East European satellite countries and still does; in Britain, for example, following the 1971 mass expulsion of Russian spies.

In 1962, a Hungarian secret police officer, Bela Lapushknyik, who knew much about KGB activities in the West, was poisoned while in Austrian police custody after he had fled from Hungary but before he could be interrogated by western services. In 1965, Canada expelled Russian diplomats who, with almost derisive lack of discretion or precautions, tried to 'buy' Canadian officials with access to industrial secrets which Russia wanted. In 1969, the Austrian scientist, Josef Eitzenberger, who worked on defence projects in West Germany, was discovered to have been supplying the KGB with NATO secrets.

The Russians launched hundreds of larger and smaller operations as they became increasingly confident and experienced in overseas espionage and contemptuous of western security procedures. This contempt was displayed when, in 1963, the KGB tried to frame American Professor Frederick Barghoorn who was then visiting Russia. It was an audacious ploy. In the United States, the FBI had just picked up three KGB officers under incriminating circumstances. Two were protected by diplomatic immunity and released. The third was operating under flimsy cover, as driver for a Soviet trade mission. The KGB believed it needed an American to trade for their incarcerated chauffeur-spy and settled on Barghoorn simply because he happened to be handy.

As he was entering his Moscow hotel one night, Barghoorn was stopped by a Russian and handed some papers, later said by the Russians to contain stolen secrets. Within seconds, waiting KGB officers grabbed him and marched him off first to the local militia headquarters, then to prison. When the KGB passed along word that they were willing to trade Barghoorn, 'the American spy', for the Russian agent in FBI custody, President Kennedy, after checking with the CIA that the professor was 'clean', dispatched an angry message to the Kremlin demanding Barghoorn's immediate release. Surprised that the American president would personally intervene, the Russians gave up their prize. The wrists of several second echelon KGB officials were slapped by their superiors for the embarrassment caused, but Soviet espionage continued to display a cavalier attitude towards risks, born of a gambler's confidence that to break even was the worst that could happen, and that much of the time the odds were just too favourable to be passed up.

At the same time, the KGB maintained its repressive procedures at home. Occasionally, it made gestures to mollify pressure groups abroad which appealed for less harsh treatment for Russian writers, intellectuals and others persecuted for expressing dissenting views. But usually it ignored such appeals.

It emerged not only as an instrument of Soviet policy, but also as a force often capable of influencing and even altering the direction such policy took. In 1964, a KGB near-fatal poison gas attack on a West German official visiting a monastery near Moscow as a tourist resulted in the cancellation of Premier Nikita Khrushchev's planned visit to Bonn, during which Khrushchev, against KGB wishes, had hoped to improve frigid Russian-German relations.

In recent years, a measure of dissatisfaction has developed in some Soviet circles over KGB activity in foreign affairs, especially after the failure of Soviet intelligence to forecast upheavals in Greece and Cyprus, where substantial Russian spy networks were deployed, or the rapprochement between Iraq, which Moscow believed it could control, and Iran, which it knew it could not. But KGB influence easily overshadows internal expressions of concern about its foreign policy involvements, particularly when it can claim, with some justification, to have helped end Portugal's status as a reliable western ally. A high ranking Czechoslovak defector to the west said detailed plans for a Communist take-over in Portugal were worked out by the Russians who controlled the Portuguese Communist Party which strongly influenced the officers who formed the junta in Lisbon after the Portuguese coup in 1974.

Although its direct influence in western trade unions is not apparent, the KGB can also claim, again with some justification, to have helped undermine the economic strength of some west European countries through those strikes, some in key industries, which were artificially provoked or prolonged because of exertions by trade union officials open to, sometimes indirect, KGB influence. It was not considered remarkable that former KGB chief Alexander Shelepin briefly became head of the Soviet Trade Union organization. It had close contact with western Communist union groupings and activists, particularly through the Communist-dominated World Federation of Trade Unions. British Labour Prime Minister Harold Wilson referred more than once to politically inspired strikes in Britain.

As for direct KGB influence in the execution of Soviet foreign policy, it is reliably estimated that three of every five Soviet diplomats stationed abroad are KGB officers on active duty, as well as a corresponding proportion of Soviet foreign correspondents and trade officials. Many Soviet officials attached to the United Nations in New York, Geneva and other cities are active KGB agents. The Russians have ignored suggestions from the American State Department that, although they have the right to send whom they like to fill positions which fall to the Soviet Union at the UN, it is wrong to send spies on active duty.

KGB officers stationed abroad as diplomats or officials can be divided into three primary categories — those engaged in gathering intelligence through monitoring publications and through other generally accepted and legitimate methods; those assigned to recruiting new personnel (preferably among officials and scientists of the countries in which they are stationed); and case officers controlling locally resident 'illegals'.

Within the last few years, the Soviet ambassadors to several countries, including Morocco, Indonesia and Afghanistan, are known to have been KGB men. More often, however, KGB agents are assigned lower diplomatic ranks, sometimes humble positions like embassy chauffeur, though he might actually outrank the ambassador in his own embassy.

The discovery and expulsion of a KGB diplomat does not end his usefulness. Yuri Novikov, expelled from Washington in 1953 for espionage activity, surfaced again thirteen years later at the Soviet embassy in London. Nikolai Savin, expelled from Switzerland in 1972, waited only two years to return to foreign duty, in Algeria. The indiscreet Lev Yatisyna was ordered to leave Zaire in 1971 and then expelled from Mali the following year.

American Communist spies who stole and passed on atomic secrets were controlled by the Soviet vice-consul in New York, Anatoli Yakovlev. Yuri Pavlenko, a diplomat at the Russian embassy in Rome ran a spy network against NATO, which included Giorgio Rinaldi, a stunt parachutist who took photographs of NATO installations in Italy while floating to Earth on his parachute after apparently innocent stunt flights.

Non-diplomatic KGB personnel, agents engaged in covert missions abroad, have also played central roles in Russian espionage operations in recent years. Rudolph Abel controlled a network of 'illegals' in the United States for almost a decade, issuing instructions and transmitting results to Moscow, while posing as a professional photographer in New York. Konon Molody, disguised as a British businessman and better known as Gordon Lonsdale, established a network for ferreting out British naval secrets. British intelligence officer George Blake was a KGB agent who passed on to the Russians details of American and British espionage operations and was responsible for the death of many western agents. Abel, Molody and Blake were finally caught. Abel and Molody were exchanged for western agents apprehended by the Russians. Blake escaped from a British prison and made his way to Russia with Russian help.

KGB Administrative Structure

A brooding, sprawling grey structure in Moscow's Dzershinsky Square, a quarter of a mile from the Kremlin, is KGB headquarters and nerve centre. There are regional headquarters throughout the Soviet Union and in major Soviet embassies abroad.

In addition to its surveillance of developments and activities within the Soviet Union, the KGB runs labour camps in which tens of thousands of persons are incarcerated, as well as other prisons, and mental hospitals for the treatment of political dissenters. It employs an estimated 100,000 persons (plus more than a quarter of a million special KGB troops deployed domestically), of whom it is believed 25,000 are engaged in planning or perpetrating espionage against other countries.

Technically, the director of the KGB is responsible to the Soviet Council of Ministers. In fact, he is answerable to the more important Politburo of the Soviet Communist Party, of which he is a key member.

There are three major, and several lesser, KGB directorates, each dealing with a specific area of KGB work. Only one, the First Directorate — devotes its energies primarily to espionage matters. The other two of the three major directorates numbered Second and Fifth as a result of shuffling of assignments and priorities over the years function primarily in the realm of domestic political police work (as do most of the lesser directorates). However, the Second Directorate also contains sections assigned to recruiting and maintaining surveillance of foreign diplomats and other visitors to the Soviet Union.

A series of First Directorate departments deals with specified geographic areas — North America, Latin America, the Middle East, China, western Europe, etc. There is frequently overlapping between these departments and between them and specialized First Directorate service sections. These service sections undertake such tasks as control of agents abroad, counter-intelligence, scientific espionage, dirty tricks, and action missions (including sophisticated sabotage, murder poison pellets were used to execute Ukrainian exiles in Munich in the late 1950s — and kidnapping, though the KGB has largely shied away from such activities in recent years).

Plans for specific operations generally originate in the regional divisions which are directly interested. They are submitted to the politburo for endorsement only if they might conflict with Soviet policy (by offending nations the Russian Foreign Ministry might be wooing) or if, through slip-up, they might provoke international incidents. If the espionage plans are consistent with basic Soviet espionage policy (obtaining foreign diplomatic, military and industrial secrets) and are unlikely to endanger Soviet diplomatic objectives, the office of the director of the KGB, or even the head of the First Directorate, can give the go-ahead. Less senior officials occasionally take responsibility for secondary operations but are generally reluctant to stick their necks out.

Once approval is obtained for an operation, the regional division involved calls first on its own resources, falling back on the services of the specialist departments for special equipment, expert advice and assistance. The scientific and dirty tricks departments originate many operations, after consultation with appropriate regional departments. There is widespread rivalry within the KGB, but poaching on the territory of other departments is frowned upon.

Synopsis

It is difficult to measure the comparative success of Russian espionage in recent years. By virtue of a controlled press and a puppet legislature in the Soviet Union, the KGB has avoided serious scrutiny, supervision or criticism at home. By virtue of Russian secret police traditions and its influential position in the Soviet hierarchy, the KGB had avoided even a hint of budgetary control. Its failures have come to light only through western sources which are usually second-hand, the information being passed on by interested individuals with points to make.

Clearly, Russian intelligence, with the notable assistance of foreign Communists (in America, Britain and elsewhere; accomplished a great deal in helping the Soviet Union acquire western military and industrial secrets immediately following the Second World War. They have been less successful so far in discovering what exactly is happening in neighbouring China, a major challenge in view of the anxiety the Russians display about the Chinese Peoples Republic and of the belief held by so many of them that, despite occasionally improved relations, a Russian Chinese war is inevitable.

6.   THE CHINESE

When Communist China was admitted to the United Nations and sent its first delegation to UN headquarters in New York in 1971, at least three senior members of that delegation were intelligence officers of long standing. However, their appointment was not a deliberate affront to the world body, nor, unlike equivalent Russian actions, was it a move to reinforce the local Chinese espionage apparatus. Despite proverbial oriental inscrutability, the reasons were much less devious. The Chinese have always believed that knowledge is strength. They have traditionally assigned extremely capable men to run their intelligence services. When men of such calibre are needed for other assignments, like manning the first Chinese UN delegation, they are seconded to these new jobs, not because they are spies, but because they are proven men of competence, though they may revert to espionage activity, even within their new roles, if circumstances require.

Despite this eminently logical approach, Chinese intelligence has, from time to time, lapsed into confusion and patterns of behaviour incongruous for a people who can claim the longest history of familiarity with the worth, ways and wiles of espionage. Acting from a perverse sense of loyalty, compounded by the survival instinct, dedicated Chinese secret agents have, in recent years, sent home reports which not only were false or irrelevant, but which they knew to be false or irrelevant. Acting on instructions, they have engaged in senseless or inadvisable acts of violence. Though these aberrations may now be a thing of the past, they indicated a degree of instability which appears to be built into the context of Communist China's 'permanent revolution'.

As has already been noted, China's connection with meticulous espionage procedures dates at least as far back as 500 BC when the philosopher Sun Tzu described in great detail both the value of military intelligence and ways in which it should be acquired. He stressed subtlety, tact and deception. The advice he offered military commanders, including the warning that 'an army without secret agents is like a man without eyes and ears', remains pertinent today. Mao Tse-Tung is known to have studied him closely.

The emphasis on intelligence gathering is a thread which runs through the fabric of Chinese history. From earliest times, Chinese rulers, both great and obscure, have believed that knowledge is power, to be acquired and to be denied an adversary. This theme was repeatedly invoked during recurring periods when China was split into several rival states and domains. Each employed secret agents to undermine its neighbours or to help create conditions in which common ground could be found to end fruitless antagonism. During periods of Chinese unity, espionage was methodically employed to keep activities and objectives of neighbouring lands under scrutiny, either for offensive or defensive purposes.

Secret societies were an early and tenacious expression of the traditional Chinese penchant for secrecy. At first, a sanctuary for religious cults, such societies developed political and nationalistic aspirations, particularly during the Mongol and Manchu dynasties, uniting groups of people opposed to prevailing authority. They often engaged in violent attacks on the instruments of power and order, and sometimes in smuggling and outright banditry (which is why traditional Chinese political terminology frequently still requires that opponents be described as bandits). In time, the secret societies grew larger and more aggressive. Such mass societies as the *Boxers* (the name is a bad translation referring to purification through fist-fighting), who rose in bloody, abortive revolt in 1900, helped pave the way for the end of foreign supremacy over China and the establishment of the Chinese Republic in 1912.

The roots of modern China's intelligence services can be traced to the political confusion after the collapse of the Manchu Empire. War lords and local political leaders built small empires of their own and fielded agents to discover ways to extend their influence, power and wealth. In the early 1920s, Russian support for Sun Yat-sen's efforts to unify the country, expressed through agents sent by Moscow to assist Sun's regime, set the stage for close relations between Chinese Nationalist leaders and the Kremlin. These were severed when Chiang Kai-shek, Sun's heir and successor, became convinced that the Russian intention was to dominate China, a view later to be inherited by the Chinese Communists after they had seized power.

Secrecy as Normal Procedure

The Chinese can be said to be the originators of the 'need to know' syndrome. Over the centuries, the habit of secrecy and concealment of activities and intentions have become so deeply implanted, that the lines between Chinese official intelligence procedures and normal government performance are thin indeed, as any diplomat or correspondent who has served in Peking can testify. Acquiring and using intelligence is considered part and parcel of governing, as is the concealment of even the most innocent information concerning government activity, unless sound purpose can be served by disclosure.

Inevitably, a culture so obsessed with secrecy goes to great lengths to conceal details of its espionage machinery, the mystery surrounding which is maintained also by the fact that the Chinese have not been nearly as plagued as the Russians by defections abroad; nor have they been afflicted, as the American intelligence establishment has been, by a spate of exposes by former espionage operatives.

From time to time, snippets circulate about the function, increased authority or depreciation of one Chinese intelligence bureau or another. But much of what is revealed appears to be for internal consumption, motivated by moves marking an unceasing power struggle within upper echelons of the Chinese leadership. The only certainty is that the Social Affairs Department, the intelligence unit of the Chinese Communist Party, wields ultimate authority over other Chinese espionage organizations. These include the Central External Liaison Department, which deals mainly with acquiring and evaluating intelligence concerning other countries; military intelligence, which deals with strategic problems and weaponry; and the intelligence branch of the Ministry for Public Security, which deals primarily with domestic political policing. Various other administrative bodies, including the Foreign Ministry and the Ministry of Trade, have their own intelligence units as well. The operations, organizational strength and importance of each of these are subject to the uncertain political climate within China.

The Communist Party's Social Affairs Department had its origins in the development of the party in the Chinese hinterland in the 1920s and 1930s, and was moulded in the struggle for mastery of China between the Communists and the Nationalists, which ended in 1949 with the Nationalist defeat and retreat to the island of Formosa. The agency came to terms with the outside world during China's subsequent strivings to stake a claim as a major power, a development marked by frequent fumblings and occasional tantrums, including the manhandling of Russian diplomats in Peking, and Chinese embassy staff in London threatening British police with staves.

The first task of the Social Affairs Department after the Communist take-over was to unearth and destroy counterrevolutionary plots, primarily those devised (sometimes with CIA direction or assistance) by Nationalists based in Formosa, or across the border in Burmese mountain sanctuaries. Simultaneously, the agency set about constructing networks of agents in 'overseas' Chinese communities, in southeast Asia, Indonesia, the United States and Britain.

Victory over the Nationalists had convinced Communist leaders that many other parts of Asia were ripe fruit ready to tumble into the Communist barrel. Revolutionary movements in Malaya, Thailand, Burma and Vietnam were given active support by Chinese agents, moving surreptitiously into what Peking believed should be its unchallengeable sphere of influence. A team of operatives was dispatched to, and recruited in, Tibet before Chinese troops moved in to seize control of the country in 1959. Others had been sent to India, even before the end of the brief period of close friendship between Peking and New Delhi which was transformed into open antagonism when the Chinese concluded that India, probably allied to Russia, would contest its objective of supremacy in Asia.

The China-Russia Split

Xenophobic by habit, the Chinese leaders had always been suspicious of their Russian allies, with whom they share a six thousand-mile border as well as an ideology. Chinese mistrust has not been based on imaginary factors. The worker-oriented Marxism of Russian dogmatism clashed with the peasant-oriented Marxist theology of the Chinese leaders. Stalin had long believed that the Chinese Communist view of historical forces could never lead to victory over the Nationalists and Moscow tried to impose its own beliefs and agents on the Chinese revolutionary movement. The Chinese Communists never forgave the Russians this lack of faith (and ideological impurity). Nor were they pleased by comparatively meagre economic and technological assistance they were to receive from the Soviet Union after they emerged victorious, at a time when the huge assistance rendered through the United States Marshall Plan was saving Western Europe from economic disaster.

The break between the two Communist giants was slow in coming, but when it came it was devastating. Chinese intelligence services were, thereupon, given what has since been their primary assignment — to determine Soviet intentions with regard to China (Soviet intelligence services have repeatedly planted rumours of Russian plans to knock out China's nuclear military capacity) and to counter Soviet influence in areas of Chinese interest.

In the Middle East and particularly in Africa, agents, generally under diplomatic cloak or officially representing the New China News Agency, were deployed to claim for Peking the position of leader of the world's developing nations and to picture the Soviet Union as self-seeking and wicked. The task was a new one for Chinese agents, many of whom had never before ventured beyond their country's borders. Their skills were not always up to the job.

They strongly supported an abortive plot by Arab revolutionaries in 1965 to assassinate Egyptian President Gamal Abdul Nasser, the most popular Arab leader in modern times.

The failure of the attempt was followed by the hasty and

humiliating departure of the Chinese ambassador from Cairo. Chinese diplomats were also named as organizers of coups which misfired in Kenya and Malawi. The Chinese were publicly accused of sedition in Zambia, the Central African Republic and Dahomey, all of which had previously extended diplomatic recognition to Peking. These clumsy plots seemed to justify the attitude of those African nations which had withheld recognition.

Faulty Chinese intelligence in Africa, stimulated by revolutionary zeal, was responsible for the worst blunder of all. While visiting East Africa in 1964, Premier Chou En-lai, a man too wise to make pronouncements in foreign places without expert guidance, declared 'the time is ripe for revolution in Africa'. These words were hardly welcome to African leaders who had struggled to overcome divisive elements in their countries, only to see them stirred up once more by a foreign visitor who claimed to know more about their lands than they did themselves. Several African nations soon severed diplomatic ties with Peking. The Chinese government was required to draw heavily on its limited supply of foreign reserves to distribute aid to African countries and demonstrate that it really was not seeking to undermine them. More cautious and correct subsequent Chinese dealings with African governments showed that Peking had learned an expensive lesson.

Although Chou's pronouncement was probably the result of faulty intelligence gathering and evaluation by inexperienced operatives, much that went wrong with Chinese intelligence during the 1960s was the product of another factor. During the so-called Cultural Revolution, when China was in a state of internal upheaval and Chinese were called upon to demonstrate their revolutionary fervour, intelligence administrators and agents were as much affected as academics, factory managers and local bureaucrats, many of whom were sent to work on farms to refresh their revolutionary dedication. China took flight from reality in search of the ideological purity its leaders demanded; its functionaries did the same.

Instead of reporting developments their government should have known, instead of taking an accurate reading of the international climate as it might have affected Chinese interests, agents, who through experience had come to know how properly to follow their trade, began concentrating on exercises meant only to demonstrate that their Marxist faith remained undefiled by foreign contact. Reports were often devoted to claptrap about ideological backwardness or inevitable collapse of non-Communist or 'revisionist' Communist nations, propaganda that could just as easily have been hacked out in Peking. Trained overseas spies spent their time compiling 'information' which they believed their superiors in Peking wished to receive. Though much of it made a mockery of both their jobs and the truth, it was designed with another objective in mind, to satisfy the prevailing revolutionary hysteria. Nevertheless, many agents were summoned home for ideological cleansing through manual labour in factories and on farms, while others openly engaged in activities abroad which were totally contrary to the principles of tact and discretion which the Chinese had long considered the hallmark of the practice of espionage.

Among their more extreme operations was an incident in The Hague, in 1966, when, with little attempt at concealment, they kidnapped an injured Chinese — apparently a would-be defector to the West whose wounds they had inflicted from a Dutch hospital to which he had been taken by the police for treatment. The kidnapped man was spirited away to a Chinese diplomatic building in the Dutch capital where it was soon announced by the Chinese that he had died. The incident enraged public opinion in the Netherlands and severely strained Dutch Chinese relations.

A New Conundrum

The Cultural Revolution had been launched by Mao-Tse-tung to avert what he believed to be the danger that China might lose its revolutionary élan, as Russia had, and become soft and flabby before it had overcome the burdens of history and emerged as a major world power. But the confusion it produced within China was dangerous to national unity, particularly in view of growing antagonism with the Soviet Union and the Chinese conviction that Russia's goal was to dominate Peking. Convinced it had served its purpose in refreshing China's spirit, Mao called off the Cultural Revolution (though possibly only temporarily, he warned) and Chinese agents again set about their tasks without having to look over their shoulders for those ready to denounce them as corrupted.

Moves to revolutionize Africa were replaced with carefully plotted efforts to block Russian advances there. It was not, and is not, a simple assignment, in view of the contrast between Russia's and China's ability to distribute financial and technical assistance. In some cases, Chinese agents in African capitals found themselves largely confined to tracking down and publicly identifying African personnel recruited by the KGB.

In Asia, Chinese basic policy turned towards isolating India as well as blocking Soviet advances. This has presented the Chinese with complications they still have not resolved, because their natural allies were not revolutionaries who sought to overthrow established non-Communist governments in Southeast Asia and other parts of the continent but comparatively right-wing Pakistan and even the United States. Unable, for ideological reasons, to embrace the American connection, the Chinese were often reduced to adopting a low profile, though compelled to offer token support to revolutionaries while their secret agents did little more than report on developments.

In less than a decade, the Chinese had moved from the specific to the general, concerned less with the ideological content of foreign governments than with their own long-term strategic problems. The most dramatic expression of this transformation has been in Western Europe, considered by Peking potentially its major ally against the Russian threat. A key assignment for Chinese agents in the West is to keep watch on KGB activities there and, where it seems advisable, to pass word on to western intelligence services. Unconfirmed reports say that, in the early 1970s, Chinese agents handed the CIA details of a KGB plot to smear United States Secretary of State Henry Kissinger as a KGB agent.

A new generation of Chinese leaders who are soon to assume command may make basic changes in policy, but an indication of the Chinese conundrum is their apparent quandry in using opium as a weapon against the West. At the height of the war in Vietnam, Chou En-lai admitted that Chinese opium was being sent for distribution among American troops, and indeed the drug problem among American forces in Vietnam became a serious matter. But it is known that narcotics were shipped in by non-Communist and non-political sources in Southeast Asia as well, because of the vast profits available from the drug trade. Furthermore, it is believed that, though the Chinese continued (and possibly continue) to market small quantities of narcotic drugs (largely to finance overseas operations and, perhaps, recruit 'illegals'), they have grown concerned about the possibility that the trade might get out of hand, be used for domestic consumption and undermine the Communist revolution.

While the impact of long-term strategic problems has rattled administrators of China's overseas espionage operations, no such uncertainty plagued Chinese domestic intelligence operations and corresponding political police work. Their continued efficacy has been manifested by the absence of serious divisions in the country, even during the course of the Cultural Revolution upheaval. There were reports of local military commanders attempting to construct regional power bases outside Peking's control, but they appear to have been short-lived efforts, quickly suppressed by Communist leaders.

Most intriguing is the case of Lin Piao, Minister of Defence and generally acknowledged heir to Mao. His death in 1971 remains a mystery. Deliberately leaked stories told of his attempted flight to the Soviet Union during which he died when his plane was shot down by pursuing Chinese Air Force jets. Whatever form his death took, it seems evident that Lin Piao, apparently tiring of waiting to assume Mao's mantle, planned a coup — perhaps involving the assassination of the Chinese leader which was uncovered and foiled by Chinese domestic intelligence operatives before it could be activated. In view of Lin Piao's seniority and central position within the Chinese hierarchy and military establishment, as well as his long experience with political intrigue, the domestic intelligence apparatus displayed a refined degree of alertness and efficiency in bringing about his downfall.

The Agents

Chinese intelligence services abroad are largely staffed and directed by personnel of Chinese diplomatic missions, supplemented by personnel of the expanding New China News Agency. The proportion of Chinese diplomats and foreign correspondents who are spies can only be guessed at (more than half would be an informed guess). Recruits from 'overseas' Chinese communities — New York and San Francisco's Chinatowns and London's Gerrard Street, for example — serve as 'illegals' and provide the third primary source of China's secret agents beyond the country's borders.

Whether for reasons of racial pride or xenophobia, the Chinese apparatus, unlike most other espionage services, has always been extremely reluctant to trust important intelligence positions or assignments to foreigners. With certain exceptions, this suspicion extends even to westerners who have openly rallied to the Chinese Communist cause. Many of those who migrated to China found themselves imprisoned during the Cultural Revolution and subsequently urged to return to their homes in the West. Those who have made friendly overtures to Chinese diplomatic missions abroad have often been suspected by the Chinese of being Russian agents and either spurned or treated with frigid correctness.

Among the non-Chinese who have played notable roles in the history of Chinese espionage are Michael Borodin, representative of the Russian-dominated Comintern (Communist international), who maintained a link between Chinese Nationalist and Russian leaders during the late 1920s, and English-born Morris 'Two-Gun' Cohen, who was an aide to both Sun Yat-sen and Chiang Kai-shek.

Borodin had been dispatched to Peking to influence Chinese Nationalist thinking along Soviet lines. Despite some success in infiltrating Communists into positions of influence in Nationalist ranks, he found Chiang Kai-shek increasingly attracted to American attachments and angered by Stalin's efforts to intervene in Chinese affairs. There was little to indicate at the time (Borodin was summoned back to Moscow in 1927) that the smallish Chinese Communist Party, soon to be decimated by Chiang Kai-shek, would come to power two decades later.

Cohen's involvement in Chinese affairs was more significant at the time. While a young man in Edmonton, Canada, he had rushed to the assistance of a Chinese who was being mugged. As a result of subsequent developments, he became close to Chinese people in the town and met Sun Yat-sen who, shortly after, visited Chinese communities in the United States and Canada and who asked Cohen to be his bodyguard on the tour, This led to a long association, during which Cohen acted as Sun's business agent abroad before going to China to become one of the key advisers there on military affairs during the Nationalist reign. He was the first to alert the Chinese to the threat posed by growing Japanese militarism. He was also an active intelligence adviser, helping the Chinese government cope with Communist, war lord and pirate threats during the late 1920s and early 1930s.

The possibility of a foreigner now exercising the same influence in Chinese intelligence matters is inconceivable. Aside from the confident re-emergence of efficient, experienced intelligence cadre in the land where the value of intelligence was first recognized, someone not intimately familiar with the uncertainty of the Chinese political climate, and the potential for sudden reverses of policy direction, would be unable to cope with the assignment.

7.   THE BRITISH

'The extension of British rule throughout the world... to... render wars impossible and promote the best interests of humanity... — such was the dream of Cecil Rhodes who, towards the close of the 19th century, sought to raise the Union Jack over ever wider regions of southern Africa. But the establishment of *Pax Britannica* was the objective of military men and merchants, rather than of British intelligence whose exploits, though often spectacular and historic, have been largely confined over the centuries to protecting already established British interests, rather than extending Britain's domain and influence.

There were occasional forays into broader areas of endeavour, including the harnessing of foreign nationalist forces to British objectives and the clandestine assault on the heart of a revolution in a distant country. But such operations were few in number and usually limited in scope. By the closing quarter of the 20th century, British intelligence had adopted exclusively a defensive posture. The impulses which had produced ambitious deeds in Arabia and Moscow had apparently been washed away by the tides of time.

The first recorded deployment of spies in Britain was in Roman times. Julius Caesar, preparing the initial Roman thrust into Britain, dispatched Commius, a Gallic tribal chief, to sound out and scout out related tribes already settled in England. Caesar also dispatched a Roman officer for preliminary coastal reconnaissance. Both these missions were failures the tribes which gathered to greet Caesar when he landed with his legions were unexpectedly fierce and almost drove the Romans off before they could establish a beach-head, and the landing beach chosen by Caesar's naval scout, near Deal in Kent, was so exposed that the Roman ships were badly battered by the first storm that blew up. Later, Roman intelligence relied more on spies recruited from among native British tribes and proved more accurate.

More effective than Caesar's excursions into the realm of espionage in Britain were those of William the Conqueror's half-brother, Bishop Odo, eleven centuries later. Odo, who was later to be imprisoned for treason, deployed his priests as an information gathering service, to keep Norman overlords informed of the mood and temper of their subjugated Anglo-Saxon flocks. But problems inherent in national development in Britain then, and for a long time thereafter, militated against the development of a coordinated intelligence system. Individuals were encouraged by rewards to offer useful information about adversaries to one sovereign or another. Bounty-hunting became a profession, particularly when informants were given a portion of the possessions of secret enemies they incriminated, a practice increasingly common after religious unrest and heresy spread in the 14th century to herald the Reformation.

Thomas Cromwell, Henry VIII's principal secretary, was the first notable name in the history of British intelligence. When Henry declared himself head of the English church, after the Pope refused to sanction his divorce from Catherine of Aragon, Cromwell became his instrument for seeking out and rooting out monastic influence in England, a process involving the establishment of a widespread informer system. His eventual demise may have resulted from the faultiness of some of the information he offered the king about other matters. Arranging the marriage between Henry and Anne of

Cleves, he presumed to assure the king, who had never seen his intended bride, that Anne was beautiful when, in fact, she was not. Nor was his contention that the marriage was politically advisable borne out by subsequent developments. The king's faith in Cromwell's judgment was shattered and lie raised no objection when Cromwell was later accused of high treason and executed.

No such error was committed by Sir Francis Walsingham, Elizabeth I's spymaster, the founder of modern espionage.

Walsingham set up networks of agents, at home and abroad, to protect his queen and England against domestic and foreign intrigues and conspiracies. He made extensive use of double agents and cryptography, transforming espionage into a comprehensive system which, among its other accomplishments, prevented the Spanish Armada, which was designed to destroy England's power, from ever becoming more than a vain threat.

But with the death of Walsingham at the end of the 16th century, the espionage apparatus he had constructed was allowed to fall into disuse and decay. No one with adequate imagination and skill emerged to sustain it; nor were adequate funds made available. Intelligence gathering in Britain again became the province of unorganized informants. It required the emergence of a leader of the zeal and imagination of Oliver Cromwell, the anti-royalist Lord Protector of England, to reintroduce an effective intelligence apparatus in the 17th century. John Thurloe was appointed its administrator, was given adequate funds for the job, and dedicated himself to uncovering and undermining royalist plots, a task he performed with a thoroughness even Walsingham would have envied.

Thurloe drew an effective security curtain around Cromwell and planted spies in foreign circles so efficiently that an Italian diplomatic intriguer stationed in London wrote home that '...no government on earth... divulges its affairs less than England, or is more punctually informed of those of others'. Plots to reclaim the throne for exiled King Charles were known in London as soon as they were laid, and conspirators were apprehended before their conspiracies went beyond the planning stage. Royalist communications were intercepted, as were smuggled weapons intended for use against Cromwell. Thurloe also divided England into regions to facilitate what was, in effect, a system of political policing. But this enraged the populace and was soon abandoned.

Military to the Fore

As with Walsingham, after Thurloe's departure, organized British intelligence crumbled and the informant system again flourished, supplemented by occasional paid agents on specific missions. Systematic intelligence gathering became largely an instrument of military activity, with commanders, particularly those in the field, the prime manipulators of 'intelligencers'. The best known British spy of the American Revolution wasn't a professional agent at all; merely a military officer carrying out his assignment. Major John Andre was sent to consult with General Benedict Arnold, commander of the American fortress (and later military academy) at West Point. Arnold, disgruntled because of what he considered insufficient recognition of his daring exploits on behalf of the revolutionary cause, had decided to turn coat and was prepared to deliver West Point to the British for a handsome reward. After arranging details for the British seizure, Andre, in mufti, was stopped by American militiamen on his way back to his own lines. Mistaking them for British soldiers, he revealed his identity persuasively enough to prevent his subsequent bluffing efforts from being convincing. He was taken prisoner and later executed, despite British anger that an officer on a mission to which he had been invited by an American general, albeit a treacherous one, should so be dealt with.

By that time, British ministers had again begun to recognize the potential usefulness of organized intelligence and were again prepared to allocate funds for a national espionage service. During the French Revolution, which was soon followed by a war between Britain and France, spies on assignment kept London informed of developments on the other side of the English Channel. British agents were also often involved in counter-revolutionary uprisings in France. During the subsequent Napoleonic confrontation, when the French emperor tried to cripple England by blockading it, the British not only managed to break the blockade, partly through the acquisition of information on how it was being run, but also extracted information on Napoleonic strategy from bribable sources within the emperor's court in Paris and from venal French and other diplomats elsewhere in Europe.

During the Napoleonic wars, the Duke of Wellington developed Britain's first organized military intelligence system, with officers specifically trained in spying and evaluation procedures. But the emergence of a unified Germany, dominant on the continent, in the late 19th century truly concentrated British attention on the formidable defence questions that had to be answered if British security was to be guaranteed. It was realized in London that more methodical espionage procedures would have to be developed than those which had been employed by Britain since Thurloe's departure from the scene. The intentions and plans of foreign governments had to be more carefully monitored. The capabilities of potentially hostile foreign military forces had to be studied.

Britain already had the makings of a counter-espionage service. The Special Irish Branch (later to be the Special

Branch) of Scotland Yard had been established to cope with Irish revolutionaries who attempted, through bomb attacks and other acts of terror, to gain independence for Ireland. The Special Branch was also to keep watch over European socialist revolutionaries (who were to number Marx and Lenin in their ranks) and anarchists who congregated in London in the last half of the 19th century and early in the 20th century.

But the increasingly frequent and ominous clash of national interests between European powers prompted a closer look in London at MO 2 — the skeleton of a military intelligence system which had come into being over the years. MO 2 stood for Military Operations, Section 2. There were six sections in all, the others dealing with various aspects of military administration and strategy. MO 5 was a catch-all bureau, established to take on special duties as they arose.

In 1909, the Imperial Defence Committee decided almost casually that it should take responsibility for counter-espionage. Captain Vernon Kell, a young officer, was given a small office and instructed to get on with the job — by himself. Though it could easily have been otherwise, Kell was bright and resourceful. He drew up careful but ambitious guidelines for his lonely bureau and when, a year later, he was authorized to recruit a small staff, he was ready to lay the groundwork for one of the most successful counter-espionage organizations the world has ever known.

MO 5 (later to be known as MI 5) established its reputation early in the game. As British-German antagonism escalated prior to the First World War, its agents followed a suspected German spy to a London barbershop, which turned out to be a 'post office', receiving and passing on both instructions from Berlin for agents in Britain and messages from the agents to headquarters in Berlin. Keeping the 'post office' and its suspicious visitors under scrutiny, MO 5 men were able to crack and wind up Germany's most important spy ring in Britain as soon as the war broke out. In the process, they perfected some of the fine points of counter-espionage procedure. At the same time, the agency inaugurated a system of recruiting civilian experts for temporary emergency service that was to provide British intelligence with an impressive collection of scientific, professional and academic brains in two world wars.

By 1912, with MO 5 still to prove its worth, a bureau was set up to coordinate the activities of British agents abroad — which meant, in effect, to construct an agency for the acquisition of foreign intelligence. It was the seed from which SIS, the Secret Intelligence Service, more commonly known as MI 6, was to grow. (Both MI 5 and MI 6 were later removed from military command and taken over directly by the government, with the prime minister ultimately responsible for the security services. This development was matched by the creation of new intelligence sections within each of the military services. Their jobs were confined to military matters, but obviously there has been overlapping with MI 6, in which case MI 6 has taken precedence. MI 5 and MI 6 were officially renamed DI 5 and DI 6 recently, but the new designations are rarely invoked outside official usage.)

The First World War

The rebirth of systematic British intelligence was marked by several extraordinary accomplishments in the First World War, two of which are particularly memorable. One, involving Lawrence of Arabia, helped change the face of the Middle East. The other altered the course of the war and, thereby, the course of subsequent history.

Thomas Edward Lawrence, Lawrence of Arabia, went into the desert as a junior officer in military intelligence to keep alive a revolt by Arab tribesmen against the Turks, who were allied to the Germans in the war. Instead of proving just a minor irritant to the Turks, Lawrence became personal leader of a major Arab uprising which tied down great numbers of Turkish troops and was a significant factor in the Turkish Middle East rout. Not only did he demonstrate the enormous potentialities of harnessing rebellious people for guerrilla warfare, but he did much to stimulate the growth of Arab nationalism which, a half century later, was to prove a mighty force in international affairs.

More immediate were the consequences of the British intelligence coup which brought the United States into the First World War and, irrevocably, onto the world stage. The United States had no desire to enter the war. President Woodrow Wilson, who had been re-elected on a neutrality platform, was anxious to mediate between the warring parties in Europe on a 'no victory for either side' basis. His country was generally antagonistic to the idea of foreign entanglements, particularly if they meant shedding American blood. No apparent vital American interests were at stake. The war was proving an industrial boon for America. There was no need to be directly involved. Nevertheless, in 1917, American troops crossed the Atlantic, went to the aid of the exhausted British and French, and contributed decisively to the German defeat the following year. They did so because of the efforts of British intelligence.

British naval intelligence had been extremely successful in breaking German military and diplomatic codes. Through genius, diligence and luck (the undetected capture of two key German codebooks), it managed to decipher great quantities of intercepted German secret messages.

Early in 1917, with the First World War dragging remorselessly on with nothing but long lists of casualties to report, British naval intelligence picked up a coded message which proved to be from Arthur Zimmermann, the German foreign minister, and to be addressed to Count Johann von Bernstorff, the German ambassador in Washington. The telegram informed von Bernstorff that Germany intended soon to unleash unrestricted submarine warfare to stop war supplies reaching Britain and France from America and other countries and that, although American vessels were likely to be sunk, efforts should be made to keep America neutral. At the same time, the message said, a move should be made to divert American attention from Europe, by offering the Mexican government an alliance with Germany and promising to help Mexico acquire Texas, New Mexico and Arizona which had once been Mexican territory. The message also suggested that Mexico, whose relations with the United States were already strained, should be urged to persuade Japan to attack the United States and extend its influence in the Pacific.

The intercepted German message was obviously political dynamite. But there was widespread suspicion in the United States of efforts by Britain to 'drag' America into the war against its wishes and interests. Disclosure of the Zimmermann telegram might be considered more of the same and be dismissed by Americans as a fabrication. Authorized by its government to bypass normal diplomatic channels, British naval intelligence, which had remained custodian of the decoded bombshell, used great tact, delicacy and substantial powers of persuasion to convince American representatives in London that the telegram was genuine. Among other things, they suggested that the Americans probably had buried in piles of automatically intercepted messages a copy of the original coded message from Berlin (one was found) and obligingly showed them how to decipher it.

Outrage exploded in the wake of the subsequent publicity

in America. The suggestion that Germany was prepared to help Mexico carve off a chunk of the United States aroused virtually unanimous indignation. Anti-German sentiment was galvanized. Wilson gave up his illusions about mediating peace in Europe and the U-boat sinkings of American vessels — no longer acceptable to Americans as part of the risks of trading with warring nations — triggered the American entry into the war. Public disclosure of the Zimmermann message had been the primary cause of America's first participation in an international dispute which did not involve exclusively its own immediate interests.

After the First World War, Britain's intelligence edifice was again largely dismantled. But it retained an organizational framework and a core of long-term objectives, as well as a small number of agents active in the field.

Sidney Reilly

Few secret agents have come closer to the image of cloak-and-dagger intrigue created by spy fiction than the extraordinary Sidney Reilly, the British spy who tried to bring down the Soviet regime shortly after the Russian Revolution. Reilly's life was one long intrigue. There is no definite proof of his origins or how he ended up.

His real name was Sigmund Rosenblum. One story has it that he was the son of Polish-Jewish parents. However, he is known to have said that he was the illegitimate son of a Russian woman, the wife of a distinguished Russian army officer in whose home he was raised, and of a Jewish doctor whose patient his mother had been. According to this story, he was 19 years old before he learned his true origins, a discovery which — in Russia's anti-Jewish climate — so shattered him that he fled in shame to South America.

There, the story continues, after a while, he signed on as a cook for an English expedition into the Brazilian jungles and, while fighting off savage Indians, saved the life of a man who happened to be a British intelligence officer. Out of gratitude and friendship, this man provided him with both passage to Britain and an introduction to British intelligence officials.

His first assignment, casually given and informally undertaken, was to report on and assess certain political developments in Europe, a task he performed with competence and perception sufficient to convince MI 6 that Reilly could be useful. But he felt strong allegiance to Russia and, prior to the First World War, having assumed a British identity and a new name, Reilly served both the intelligence services of Britain and Imperial Russia on a free-lance basis, primarily in Germany but also in Japan and other countries. However, his remarkable talents as a spy and flair for intrigue became evident after the war had begun when, adopting various disguises, he was able to acquire and pass on to Britain important German secrets, including plans for U-boat attacks on shipping. Speaking fluent German, he not only took the identity of a junior German officer, but, in that capacity, penetrated the German general staff.

Whatever loyalty he had to the Russian government crumbled with the Russian Revolution. He developed a profound hatred and contempt for the ruling Bolsheviks and was delighted when Prime Minister Lloyd George, acting on the advice of MI 6, authorized his dispatch to Moscow to undermine its new Communist rulers in the hope that Russia, under a different regime, would re-join the battle against Germany from which the Communists had withdrawn.

In Russia, Reilly quickly re-established contact with old friends, some of whom had taken on Bolshevik identities for reasons of survival and one of whom had managed to become a high official in the Bolshevik intelligence and terror organization, *Cheka.* In the early months of the Revolution,

Moscow and all of Russia were in turmoil. Many things which were later to seem improbable were then possible. Reilly devised fantastic plots. He planned to arrest Lenin and the other Bolshevik leaders at an important government meeting. He tried to bribe the bodyguards of the new government leaders to be less than vigilant. He made arrangements for establishing a new Russian government, to include men in Moscow he knew to be anti-Bolshevik. Adopting various disguises and pseudonyms, and using a *Cheka* pass his friend in the *Cheka* had given him, he flitted about probing for Bolshevik vulnerability and building anti-Bolshevik cells.

But the *Cheka* was active as well and the failure of some of Reilly's intrigues resulted from its infiltration of some of his cells. Other plots went wrong because of the impatience of some of the anti-Bolsheviks. The plots which misfired increased *Cheka* vigilance, diminishing the prospects of the others. When Social Revolutionary Dora Kaplan shot and seriously wounded Lenin late in 1918, a massive *Cheka* terror campaign was unleashed. Hundreds were executed in Moscow and Petrograd. British diplomat-spy Bruce Lockhart was arrested — and only released after the British had imprisoned the Soviet representative in London in retaliation.

With the *Cheka* on his heels, Reilly hurried to Petrograd, bribed his way aboard a merchant ship there and made his way back to England. Shortly after his return, he was awarded the Military Cross for his efforts on behalf of MI 6.

But Reilly's involvement with Russia was far from over. His hatred of the Communist regime there undiminished, he became active in organizing and supporting movements in many countries dedicated to the overthrow of the Communists. This activity involved him with an organization called 'The Trust', a clandestine group of Russians in Western Europe and Russia, some believed to be in important government positions in Moscow, who were planning a coup against the Soviet government. The possibility that 'The Trust' could actually bring about the elusive counter-revolution excited Reilly, for whom a life of tranquillity and security appeared to be anathema. He crossed back into Russia from Finland in 1925 and discovered what many, including Reilly himself, suspected — that 'The Trust' was the creation of Soviet intelligence. Reilly was never heard from again.

There were reports that he was shot immediately. However, there were also reports that he was seen alive and well in Russia as late as the 1940s. Suggestions were inevitably made that under torture or to save his life, Reilly provided the Russians with a wealth of information about British intelligence procedures and personnel. But this was strongly doubted by those who knew and worked with him.

Whatever the ultimate truth about the last chapter of Reilly's career, his adventures — and those of his British intelligence colleagues in Russia at the time — were exceptions about to prove the rule, the prelude to confirmation of a basic emphasis on defensive operations for British intelligence services. Although the SOE (Special Operations Executive) performed some spectacular acts of espionage and intelligence gathering behind German lines during the Second World War, the most remarkable wartime performances of British intelligence were in counter-espionage and, as in the First World War, in code breaking.

Ultra and Double Agents

Dwight Eisenhower, the Supreme Allied Commander, called British intelligence's so-called Ultra operation 'decisive' in determining the outcome of the Second World War. There is little doubt that it was a unique, astonishingly successful escapade which meaningfully influenced the course of the bloodiest conflict mankind had ever known.

Under the auspices of the Air Department of MI 6, a German cypher contraption, which was secretly stolen and smuggled out of Germany, was employed by skilled cryptologists to 'read' top-level German military communications, including those between Hitler and his field commanders, at the same time as those for whom the messages were meant. Ultra gave the British details of German strategy for the Battle of Britain, during which the German air force was assigned the task of knocking out British air defences as a prelude to the invasion and conquest of Britain. Information of German air attack strategy and of losses sustained by the enemy gave the British air defenders scope for careful judgment on how to deploy their inferior resources.

In the hard-fought North Africa campaigns, where the Germans had already displayed their fighting skills and strength, information obtained through Ultra on enemy deployment and intentions, helped the British withstand mighty German attacks, then box in and overwhelm the *Afrika Korps.* So much German information got through to British and American field commanders that intelligence in London felt obliged to send interceptable messages of praise to imaginary agents in occupied Europe to convince the Germans that British spies and not cryptography were the cause of their trouble.

Ultra also provided details of German deployment in France at the time of the Normandy landings in 1944 and of frenzied German troop movements as the Allied armies swept across Europe. Often the weight of numbers and strong defensive positions gave the German defenders an advantage which even accurate information could not overcome. Sometimes tightened German security kept secrets from Allied hands. Sometimes Allied commanders did not wisely use the information Ultra provided. But as the war proceeded, the

Ultra weapon proved itself over and over again, offering the Allies a comprehensive picture of what was actually happening on the battlefields while the Germans had to await the consequences of events to discover what, in fact, those events meant.

The British success with double agents, described in detail by Sir John Masterman in his report, *The Double Cross System,* was one of the most remarkable counter-espionage achievements in history. Despite the skill, experience and formidable extent of German espionage, the British were able to operate the entire German espionage system in Britain during the war without Berlin even suspecting what had happened. Not until the war was over, and captured German documents became available, was the astounding extent of the double agent operation revealed. Through it, the British had been able to achieve their objective of controlling German agents in Britain, of apprehending new 'uncontrolled' enemy spies whenever they surfaced, and of feeding the Germans false information through agents the Germans thought they themselves controlled.

The 'turned' German agents were recruited either through their basic sympathy for the Allied cause (having been compelled to enrol as German agents through threats to themselves or their families or for money) or had been genuinely loyal to Germany until convinced that, having been caught by the British, working for British intelligence was the only way they could save their lives. As newly-arrived German agents made contact with those in Britain already recruited by the British, they too were recruited or, if that seemed impossible or inadvisable, imprisoned or executed as spies.

The major problem presented by the system was that information fed back to Germany by the turned agents had to be credible. Not until victory did the British realize that they need not have worried about the possibility that other German agents, uncaught and unturned, might have been double checking faked reports on troop movements, anti-aircraft defences, civilian morale, etcetera. At times, therefore, accurate classified information was provided for the 'spies' to send back to Berlin, a painful process considered necessary if the Germans were to remain deceived and receptive to false information.

The Harder They Fall

To use an unsavoury expression of the English gentry, British intelligence 'had a good war'. In addition to its cryptological and counter-espionage coups and the work of the SOE behind German lines, it had been hugely successful in constructing spy networks in occupied Europe. It emerged from the conflict with a web of agents admirably placed to cope with Britain's next strategic confrontation — with the threat of Communist expansion in Europe under the direction of the Soviet Union. Before the end of hostilities, MI 6 began making preparations by setting up a special section to deal with Russian problems and Communist espionage. Ironically, this led to the most serious internal crisis British intelligence has ever experienced.

The man named to head the new Russian section was Kim Philby, who had been a Russian spy since the 1930s and who managed to escape detection until the late 1950s. MI 5 was successful in uncovering several important Russian agents, including the nuclear scientists Allan Nunn May and Klaus Fuchs and Russian spymaster Konon Molody who headed a naval secrets spy ring. But Philby's phenomenal success in feeding the KGB vast quantities of British intelligence secrets during the Cold War was underscored by the lengthy tenure of other Russian spies highly placed in Britain, notably Foreign

Office men Donald MacLean and Guy Burgess (both of whom fled to Moscow before they could be apprehended) and George Blake.

Blake, an important MI 6 agent, was sentenced in 1961 to an unprecedented 42 years imprisonment for serving as a Russian spy. Details of western secrets he passed on to Moscow have never been revealed — he was tried *in camera* — but at his trial, the British Lord Chief Justice declared that the damage he had done was so extreme that it had rendered much of Britain's effort 'completely useless'. The fact that the KGB was soon able to 'rescue' Blake from a British jail and spirit him away to Russia did not enhance the reputation of British security, nor did the fact that many Western secret agents were caught and executed by the Russians and East European Communist governments because of the information Blake and Philby provided them.

Suspicions were aroused and never really extinguished about the possibility that other Russian agents had infiltrated British intelligence and had not been detected. Surviving British agents in the field, particularly those of foreign nationality and those operating in Communist countries, understandably felt frighteningly exposed. Gradually, Britain's excellent post-war networks began to contract, a development hurried along by domestic economic problems which limited funds available for overseas intelligence work.

Normal operations, such as gathering intelligence through non-covert methods, through monitoring foreign publications and innocent contact with foreign officials, was maintained. British embassies abroad retained a complement of MI 6 agents. But with few exceptions, such as tracing those breaking UN-imposed economic sanctions against the rebellious former British colony of Rhodesia, British intelligence concentrated on domestic counter-espionage, particularly on rooting out Russian spies who, in the 1960s, appear to have concluded that Britain was an agreeable location for their activities. The result was the mass expulsion of Russian diplomats and trade officials — all KGB operatives — from Britain in 1971.

British intelligence now appears to be in an in-between stage, much like past periods of limbo when extraordinary accomplishment was succeeded by a shift towards the shadows of quiescence. But the traditions which produced Walsingham, Thurloe, the men who broke the Zimmermann telegram and those who ran the Ultra project are unlikely to wither away.

8. THE IMPACT OF TECHNOLOGY

In the spring of 1960, an East-West summit conference, to seek a way out of the increasingly menacing cold war, was convened in Paris and immediately fell apart. Nikita Khrushchev, then Soviet premier, stormed angrily out of the gathering, turning his back on the western leaders who had gathered for the occasion — American President Dwight Eisenhower, British Prime Minister Harold MacMillan, and French President Charles de Gaulle. Before departing, Khrushchev denounced the intrusion of an American U-2 spy plane into Soviet air space, where it had just been detected and shot down. It was, the Soviet leader said, an incident which made his participation in the summit talks unthinkable.

But this explanation for choking off a potentially momentous international exchange of views and possibly agreement was curious. The Russians were not innocents in the world of spying. They had been far more audacious in espionage activities, particularly in acquiring American atomic secrets, than any of their adversaries, and Khrushchev knew it. He knew also that the U-2 flight was not unprecedented, that high altitude American supersonic reconnaissance planes had been overflying the Soviet Union for more than a year, though never before had the Russians been able to shoot one down.

It was suggested that Khrushchev was merely being sly, that he had other reasons for not wanting to attend the Paris summit and used the U-2 incident as an excuse. But he could have found other, less explosive ways of staying away if that was his basic objective. It was not, and the mystery of his peculiar tantrum was finally unravelled by the much-underrated Swiss intelligence service, which learned that the Russians had been amazed and appalled when they inspected the wreckage of the U-2. They found the remains of aerial cameras whose sophistication and capabilities went far beyond anything they knew existed. It was their first shattering realization of how effective previous American spy plane flights must have been in charting and examining Soviet missile bases and other military installations. At the time when Khrushchev was scheduled to exchange global views with his western counterparts in the French capital, Russian military planners were in a state of shock, brought on by the realization that they simply did not know to what extent American overflights had led to a change in the strategic balance.

Like everything else, spying had become technologized over the years. Although elaborate espionage devices and gadgets had existed before the U-2, and although still more sophisticated tools for spying were already in the works, Khrushchev's dramatic exit from the Paris summit marked the moment of worldwide recognition of the technological revolution in espionage practices.

Once upon a time, a secret agent saw with his eyes and reported orally. The spies whom Genghis Khan dispatched in advance of his conquering armies were capable of covering on horseback the then astounding distance of 250 miles in a single day to deliver detailed reports on the regions and towns the Mongols were about to overrun and on the opposing forces they were about to confront. In the best traditions of heroic fiction, the Southern belle, Belle Boyd, actually dodged through Northern lines on foot during the American Civil War to reveal Northern attack plans to Southern officers. But heroic as these and other personal escapades may have been, man's engineering ingenuity had long before made its mark on the ways and means of spying, thereby diminishing the human factor.

Codes and ciphers were known to the ancient world. Invisible inks were commonly used in diplomatic communications in Renaissance Italy. Before the end of the eighteenth century, the French employed aerial espionage for military purposes. Officers equipped with spyglasses were sent aloft in the baskets of balloons, held in place above the battlefields by ropes anchored to the ground, and signalled back information on enemy positions. During the First World War, the Germans used zeppelins to keep watch on Allied maritime movements, as well as for other military purposes.

That war was, however, the occasion for a far more important development in aerial reconnaissance — the military airplane. The first war planes, flimsy flying machines, were meant exclusively for reconnaissance, to pinpoint enemy positions so that ground forces could take appropriate action. During the course of the war, reconnaissance pilots began using cameras, hand-held mechanisms, to take photographs of enemy trench lines. This was awkward and sometimes useless; the pilot had to fight the cold and the wind as well as control his plane and operate the camera. Later cameras were fixed to the body of the plane, enabling the pilot to manoeuvre more easily.

Aerial combat, which also originated in the First World War, began as a relatively ineffective counter-espionage operation. Aircraft were dispatched to prevent enemy reconnaissance planes from gathering military information on their spy flights. Pilots at first used pistols and rifles to try to shoot down intruding spy planes. Later, planes were equipped with cumbersome mounted machine guns which jammed as often as not, and later with increasingly effective weapons, a development which led to the adaptation of aircraft for bombing purposes. What started out as an innovation in intelligence gathering methods totally changed the face of war.

Each poison provokes a search for its antidote. Radar, first deployed in a significant fashion by Britain as the clouds of the Second World War began to gather over Europe, provided early warning of attacking aircraft (though its use was subsequently expanded for peacetime navigation and Cold War tracking purposes as well). Sonar and other long-range detection devices followed hard upon, including electronic sensors for detecting enemy movement in otherwise inaccessible regions. *Igloo White* sensors were among those strewn by American planes along the Ho Chi Minh trail in Vietnam to relay, to circling aircraft, signals which indicated the extent and type of traffic passing down hidden jungle roads.

The Sky Spies

Ingenious as they were, such devices for tactical intelligence gathering were far outmatched by instruments for acquiring strategic information. Perhaps the most important was the precision camera which transformed the methods of strategic planning. During the Second World War, reconnaissance planes were able to photograph wide areas for study by military analysts. But the subsequent development of high resolution and wide angle cameras as well as vastly improved photographic interpretation methods provided so much valuable information, with comparatively little risk, that serious questions were raised about the value of conventional secret agents on the ground.

The American RB-47 was able to circle the globe, refuelling in flight, at a height of 40,000 feet, with cameras capable of detecting all militarily significant installations and movement on the ground. The U-2 could soar to even greater altitudes, its long-focus cameras capable of identifying a golf ball ten miles down. Its successor, the SR-71 could cruise at Mach-3 thirty-three miles a minute — at 80,000 feet, with cameras and electronic sensors which could survey 100,000 square miles of the earth's surface in an hour. Russian *Bear, Badger* and other reconnaissance planes were similarly equipped with advanced photographic equipment and electronic devices for locking onto terrestrial communications systems and for interpreting an adversary's electronic defences. Other countries, including Britain, France and Sweden, developed sleek new aircraft for reconnaissance, or easily adaptable to that purpose.

Both the Russians and the Americans converted trawler-type vessels for espionage work, cramming them with gadgetry for monitoring land-based telecommunications and electronic defences, as well as for observing adversary naval manoeuvres. After the North Koreans seized the USS *Pueblo* in 1968 and let the Russians examine its equipment, American enthusiasm for the use of these spy ships was much reduced. They are expensive to outfit and the development of reliable spy satellites proved that much of the telecommunications interception and electronic detection work which the vessels undertook could be accomplished more safely and without the danger of provoking international incidents.

In 1960, a *Tiros* satellite was launched from Cape Canaveral in Florida and returned to earth two hours later with remarkably comprehensive photographs of vast areas of China and the Soviet Union on which experts were able to locate and identify missile sites, airfields and industrial complexes. The *Tiros* was succeeded by more sophisticated models and Russian spy satellites soon also soared up through the atmosphere to orbit the earth. Espionage had entered a new dimension and would never be the same again.

The technological revolution also had its impact on the

working habits of the conventional spy. New tools were put at his disposal. The Americans devised a silent electrically-operated poison dart gun. The Russians briefly toyed with James Bond-styled poison gas pellets to eliminate foes, including the cyanide vials used by KGB agent Bogdan Stashinsky to murder Ukrainian exile leaders Stepan Bandera and Lev Rebet in Munich in the late 1950s (Stashinsky later gave himself up and was imprisoned in West Germany).

But this sort of execution really has little to do with espionage. More to the point was the development of ever-smaller cameras for photographing documents and installations and 'night light' devices to assist in the operation. Bugging and other listening contraptions were designed for monitoring conversations and meetings. In 1960, American United Nations delegate Henry Cabot Lodge displayed a carved replica of America's Great Seal that had been presented as a gift by the Russians to the American ambassador in Moscow and which had hung in the ambassadorial office until a bugging device was discovered embedded in it. Such gadgets have now been updated to include, among other things, a laser apparatus which can pick up speech from a position outside an office or other enclosed space in which speech is taking place. At the same time, long distance, directional sound detectors and amplifiers have ended the guarantee that the discussion of top secrets out in the open, away from walls and bugs and so overworked in spy fiction, is safe from eavesdroppers.

None of this means that secrets can no longer be discussed safely. But it does mean that a new generation of security devices, scramblers, jammers and bug detectors, has had to be developed. No doubt they will have to be improved as technicians produce new model listening devices to overcome them.

9.   SPIES OF EMINENCE

1. The Master Practitioner

Every country has some kind of national security agency, to protect and promote its national interests. Such agencies, of lesser or greater dimensions and aspirations, have always existed in organized communities which had designs against, or feared the intentions of, others. Understandably, there have frequently been basically contrasting orientations — the merchant-spies of the Aztecs sought to extend Aztec power; the scouts of neighbouring tribal nations were early warning systems against the advance of Aztec warriors.

Organizational structure and operational procedure have also varied greatly. Some security agencies have long histories; others rose and fell virtually unnoticed. Even among those of lengthy tenure, some have been more effective than others. But the establishment of the first modern, comprehensive, methodical, efficient national intelligence apparatus can be identified in time and place. It can be traced to the 16th century, to the reign of Elizabeth I of England and, more specifically, to Elizabeth's spymaster, the remarkable Sir Francis Walsingham.

Prior to Walsingham, intelligence gathering, when it took place, was mostly a haphazard procedure, based on ploys, stratagems and deceptions which lacked long-term purpose or method, and which were excessively dependent on chance. Walsingham was, however, no simple contriver of new gimmicks. Nor was he merely a lucky gambler. He was an architect of a system of espionage, and the core of his system has survived the centuries. It is still widely employed by intelligence organizations large and small across the world.

Among Walsingham's lasting contributions to the art of spying was the construction of a reliable, enduring network of secret information gatherers; the methodical entrapment of individuals dangerous to his cause; the use of unsuspecting third parties to pursue his objectives; the manipulation of double agents; and the systematic use and deciphering of codes and ciphers. Just about every basic procedure employed by espionage agencies today is rooted in Walsingham's innovations four hundred years ago.

This philosopher of the cloak and dagger, this master practitioner of dubious political deeds, this efficiency expert on guile and deceit, concocted his bag of tricks under pressure. Fully to appreciate Walsingham's accomplishments, it is necessary to comprehend the political climate prevailing when he came upon the scene. England was threatened by foreign powers. It was deeply troubled by domestic sectarian antagonism between Protestants and Catholics. Mary, Queen of Scots, had made a potentially dangerous challenge to Elizabeth's right to the throne. Walsingham deployed his skills to cope with each of these problems, and contributed to the solution of all.

Intrigues, conspiracies and suspicion dominated the atmosphere, a kind of rarified air Walsingham proved eminently suited to breath. He had been recruited by Lord Burghley, Elizabeth's Secretary of State, to collate reports received from a small contingent of uncoordinated British spies on the Continent, and then to track down Catholic spies believed to be in league with foreign representatives in devising plots against behead the queen in London itself. By planting his own spies, closely monitoring the London grapevine, and receiving weekly reports from the Lord Mayor on 'all strangers who took lodgings in the city', Walsingham was kept informed of developments which fell within the province of a counterspy chief. He compiled thorough lists of persons warranting surveillance and came to Elizabeth's personal attention through his recommendation that the queen's meals be prepared and served under security conditions because of reports reaching him that attempts might be made to poison her. It was a modest beginning for the spymaster, but it hinted at his range of skills.

Burghley was impressed with the intricacy and efficiency of Walsingham's London intelligence network, and with the calibre and scope of the information it provided. The Queen was impressed with Walsingham's tact and discretion (foreign diplomats were involved) as well as with his tacit willingness to compromise on the religious question. Of stern Puritan stock, a hater of Catholics and inclined to believe no Catholic could be a loyal Englishman, he was, nevertheless, prepared to accept Elizabeth's refusal to engage in religious strife that could have led to turmoil in England.

So taken was the Queen with Walsingham's abilities and character that she dispatched him to Paris as ambassador to undertake an exceedingly delicate assignment, to overcome traditional Anglo-French antagonism and establish an alliance between the two countries. Though unable to perform this task, Walsingham did succeed in discouraging the formation of an anti-English French-Spanish alliance and in gaining greater, though not final, French acceptance of England's Protestant queen. When he left for home, after having laid the groundwork for a continental intelligence system, England had no further need to fear the threat of a concerted anti-English conspiracy by Europe's Catholic powers. In foreign affairs, it could concentrate on preparing for a conflict with Spain alone, which now seemed likely.

Return Home

In recognition of his efforts abroad and his remarkable talents, Walsingham was appointed the Queen's principal secretary when he returned to London. Using this position, and the powers it brought, he expanded his intelligence network, both in the British Isles and abroad, planting agents in the Vatican itself.

Protecting the Queen from recurring plots against her life remained his primary concern. But a national spymaster, if he properly understands his role, must have a broad view of politics and history, and Walsingham's interest in Elizabeth's personal safety was intertwined with a major policy of state — to sustain England's stability and internal peace. These, Walsingham believed, were threatened by Mary, Queen of Scots, and her claim to the throne. Mary, a Catholic, was a magnet for the sympathies of British and European Catholics. Driven from the throne of Scotland by political intrigue and her own questionable behaviour, she sought refuge in England. Elizabeth deemed it wiser to detain her rather than let her go on to the continent where Catholics might flock to her cause. Living in comfort, if not luxury, Mary was detained for 18 years, dreaming all the while of escaping her jailers and finding a way to replace Elizabeth on the throne. A number of plots were hatched by her supporters. But, by planting double agents and intercepting often coded correspondence, Walsingham made certain they foundered in their early stages.

Nevertheless, the war with Spain was growing imminent and some of Mary's supporters were growing impatient and daring. Walsingham thought in strategic terms. He was aware of the advisability of eliminating a serious though tolerable threat if other perilous situations were arising. It was time to be relieved of the tedious necessity to keep close watch on Elizabeth's rival.

A young convert to Mary's cause, Anthony Babington, had devised a plot to murder Elizabeth, free Mary and put her on the throne. Babington wanted Mary's personal approval for this scheme and, in a message smuggled to her in confinement, told her as much. Mary, reaching out for vengeance and power, gave it in writing, or so it seemed by the time Walsingham, his spies and his decipherers finished with the Babington correspondence. It has been suggested that the naive Babington led Mary into a trap laid by Walsingham. In any case, the episode was brought to a quick conclusion. Mary was beheaded.

With the throne safe from rival claimants, Walsingham turned the greater part of his attention to the more remote but more dangerous peril presented by Spain. For years, his carefully planted agents in Spain, France and Italy had reported details of a massive Spanish war fleet under construction, and of Spanish plans to use that fleet to attack, invade and conquer England. Walsingham's agents sent London a running commentary on the character and size of the Spanish Armada as it slowly took shape. They also managed to cast doubt on Spanish financial trustworthiness, thus inducing Italian bankers, who were financing much of the fleet, to force construction delays. England was, thereby, given more time to prepare.

When the Armada finally did set sail (1588), it was beaten at sea by superior English seamanship and warship design as well as the weather which battered the Spanish ships as they sought to recover from the English assault. But the basis of the Spanish disaster was the stream of secretly extracted, detailed information which permitted Elizabeth and her military commanders to expect, prepare for and meet the challenge.

In addition to being the first efficient modern spymaster, Walsingham has another claim to distinction. He is the only spymaster in recorded history who exhausted his personal fortune to supplement meagre appropriations his superior (in this case, Elizabeth) allotted for intelligence. Walsingham died respected, honoured and poor.

2. The Insatiable Ferret

Few among the many who attended the funeral of Prussian spymaster Wilhelm Stieber in 1892 were there as mourners. Stieber was an important personage and, for many, attendance at his burial was more or less mandatory. But while open rejoicing at so solemn an occasion would not have been proper, a sigh of relief rose from exalted circles throughout central Europe as the man who had helped pave the way for Germany's unity and rise to power, was lowered into his grave.

Stieber had rendered extraordinary service to the rulers of Germany, but he was also a Peeping Tom of extraordinary proportions, a skilled and tenacious snooper into private indiscretions and potentially humiliating perversities, many of which he was instrumental in compounding. Much that he learned served no purpose whatsoever. He was, nevertheless, an insatiable ferret. His life was dedicated to the acquisition of information and, though this pursuit was often arbitrary and irresponsible, his activities contributed to altering the face of Europe and transforming the art of espionage. After Stieber, spying took on new dimensions.

A Saxon by birth (1818), Stieber was directed while still a boy towards the Lutheran ministry. However, when he was a young man and living in Berlin, the capital of Prussia and soon, with Stieber's assistance, to be capital of the German Empire, he decided he had no divine calling. He gravitated towards poorer sections of the metropolis and established himself as a spokesman in law for those who inhabited its squalid semi-underworld, men and women driven by poverty and wretchedness into crime and degeneracy. Stieber was able to exploit the processes of the law with great effect in defending his impoverished clients and developed a reputation as a selfless advocate for those unable to defend themselves against the ponderous institutions of Prussian society. Few knew that while striking blow after blow in the name of justice for the socially deprived, Stieber was also a police agent, reporting to the authorities on developments in Berlin's scruffy backwaters which they believed warranted close scrutiny.

He might have spent the rest of his life working both sides of that particular market had it not been for the kind of accident more common in fiction. Despite recurring civil unrest, King Frederick William of Prussia sometimes made informal public appearances, not always with the kind of bodyguard which prevailing moods made advisable. One day, the king found himself threatened by a hostile mob. Stieber, who happened to be present, rushed to the king and, pretending to threaten him, assured him that he was well-protected and helped spirit him away. Whether his action saved Frederick William from attack is debatable. But the king thought it did, bestowed favours upon his rescuer and, in time, had him appointed commissioner of police in Berlin.

No longer required to conceal his ambitions behind a facade of public defender, Stieber expanded his search for subversive elements and dropped all preteens of concern about the underprivileged. He even went off to London for a close look at the activities of radical German exiles there, including Karl Marx. But his attention was not reserved exclusively for revolutionaries and liberals. He believed in dossiers and details, as much as he could gather about as many individuals as possible, including many Prussian dignitaries who were generally considered above suspicion. This resulted in the acquisition of an impressive collection of distinguished enemies who thought of him as an impudent, unsavoury upstart. When his protector, Frederick William, was forced by a deteriorating mental condition to vacate the throne, Stieber prudently left Prussia and took temporary employment assisting the Russian secret service.

Fate of Nations

Germany consisted at the time of a cluster of independent states. The largest was Prussia, but neighbouring Austria and France also exercised strong influence within the German realm, a situation which the new Prussian chancellor, Prince Otto von Bismarck, found intolerable. When it became apparent that Bismarck was determined to make Prussia the dominant power in Europe as well as in Germany and, in the process, crush growing liberal movements, Stieber made contact with him to offer his services. Familiar with the skills of the former information scavenger of Berlin, and recognizing the value of intelligence, Bismarck was interested. He invited Stieber back into the fold of the Prussian bureaucracy and dispatched him to Austria to learn what he could of Austrian military prowess.

Unwilling to trust the success of the assignment to subordinates, Stieber acquired a horse and cart and personally set off on his espionage mission disguised as a peddler, hawking religious trinkets or pornographic sketches, depending on his assessment of those he came across. A good judge of character and possessing the gift of gab, he was welcomed wherever he went. He saw for himself and had little trouble extracting answers for seemingly innocent queries about garrisons and military installations.

By the time he returned to Berlin, he had compiled a thorough and detailed picture of Austria's military strength and deployment. Bismarck's generals employed this information with devastating affect, bringing the Austro-Prussian War, precipitated by Bismarck, to a triumphant conclusion in a mere three weeks.

The victory excluded Austria from the arena of German affairs and permitted Bismarck to turn his attentions to France and to the establishment of the German Empire as the dominant power in Europe. It also firmly established Stieber in his role as German spymaster, though proud Prussian aristocrats who were compelled to associate with him regarded him with disdain and contempt.

Stieber swallowed their unconcealed dislike and proceeded with his preparations for Bismarck's war with France. He spent more than a year there, personally scouting the terrain. More important, however, he constructed the most massive army of spies the world had ever known. For the first time in history, espionage agents were recruited in great numbers from the ranks of the common people — shopkeepers and waiters, chambermaids and farmers, people who lived ordinary lives and never expected to be enrolled in a massive underground apparatus. Some he paid; some he blackmailed after acquiring details of indiscretions or minor crimes. From these agents, Stieber received a vast flow of bits of information which he pieced together into a coherent picture.

By the time Bismarck was again ready for war, Stieber had also prepared a comprehensive topographical analysis of France for Prussian strategists to study. They were given details of all major roads and bridges which Prussian troops were likely to cross. Stieber had also drawn up maps of cities and towns and inventories of available livestock for foraging on possible lines of march. From his more professional agents, he had gathered information on French military units, their strength and the character of their officers. Though it subsequently became the aim of all major national intelligence services to prepare such contingency information, Stieber's was the first thorough strategic map of a country that was about to be invaded.

His activity was, however, still not confined to the theatre of espionage. He kept close watch at home in Berlin, and elsewhere in Germany, reviving his old practice of compiling dossiers for possible future use. The Prussian elite was impressed and horrified by his thoroughness. But his accomplishments overrode their concerns, especially after the Prussian victory over France. Stieber convinced German leaders that his efforts were directed towards protecting the lives of the emperor and his ministers, and German interests throughout Europe.

His last major operation, when he was an old man, was the notorious *Green House* he opened and ran in Berlin. Its doors were always open to distinguished officials and others lured there by a variety of not commonly available sexual opportunities, designed to evoke perversions if none existed before.

Through discreet blackmail of *Green House* guests, Stieber was able to gather still more information for his dossiers. He died feared and hated.

3. *The Spy by Accident*

Many an untrained amateur has found himself suddenly skulking across the stage of espionage. Many have stumbled into spying through being at the right place, at the right time, with the proper qualifications and sufficient dedication. Such a man was Henri Le Caron, the British secret agent who undermined whatever chance militant Irish-Americans might have had of touching off an Irish rebellion against England towards the end of the 19th century.

It is doubtful whether the Fenians would have succeeded

even if Le Caron had never existed. The time of Ireland's independence was still a half-century off. But his story has a distinct place in the annals of espionage. It is a glimpse into the use of secret agents to neutralize conspiratorial movements operating from third countries, a not uncommon phenomenon over the ages. Both before and after the Russian Revolution, Russian spies were infiltrated into Russian exile movements abroad to learn their secrets and divert them from their objectives. As many Latin American coups have sprouted from plans laid outside the countries involved as have been hatched within their borders; as a consequence, Latin American security services are particularly active in neighbouring lands. It was into just such a political circus that Henri Le Caron stumbled.

His real name was Thomas Beach and he never did learn to speak French. Born in Colchester, England, in 1841, Beach was restless by nature, even as a boy. He neither completed his schooling nor mastered a trade. Smitten by wanderlust, he turned up in Paris before he was twenty years old with little money and even less idea of what he was after. He supported himself through jobs arranged with the help of English people he met in the French capital.

Also among his friends there were a number of Americans who, when the American Civil War started in 1861, returned home to answer the call to colours. Still footloose, Beach decided to cross the Atlantic too and, seeking adventure, he enlisted in the Northern army as soon as he arrived in the United States. Wanting to spare his parents possible anguish if anything happened to him, he pretended to be French and joined up under the name Henri Le Caron, the name he was to use for the rest of his life.

Though he had been unable previously to persevere in any pursuit for long, army life suited Le Caron. He contentedly spent the next four years in uniform, much of it in combat, rising from private to the rank of lieutenant. His new identity and army life proved so personally rewarding that, after the war, he decided to remain in America and joined various veteran organizations. Filled with pompousness and dreams of glory, some of these organizations were prone to distribute honorary military ranks to their more active members. Lieutenant Le Caron was quickly promoted to major in the so-called Grand Army of the Republic.

Though he was still in his mid-twenties, the war had somewhat subdued this fidgety, wandering Englishman. Had other factors not intervened, he might have settled down to devote the rest of his life exclusively to a newly-acquired ambition, to study and practice medicine. Indeed, he was soon to embark on such a career and to become successful at it. But his new maturity prompted him to do something that was, unexpectedly, to direct his life in a completely different direction. He decided to re-establish contact with his parents whom he had neglected since leaving England. He started writing to his father — long, affectionate, descriptive letters which recounted all he had gone through since leaving home. It was those letters which were to launch Le Caron into a career of espionage.

Among his fellow officers in the army had been John O'Neill who, in the course of many conversations, had described to Le Caron the hopes of many Irish-Americans to drive the English out of Ireland and, more immediately, to conquer Canada through military action. Canada, O'Neill had said, could be a base of operations against England. Among other things, its ports could be used to dispatch privateers to disrupt English shipping and thus bring the English government to its knees.

Le Caron did not attach much seriousness to these plans

but, in the letters he wrote his father, he described at length what O'Neill had said. Unlike his son, Le Caron's father was very disturbed by Fenian intentions — as so often, the Irish Question was a major English anxiety at the time. The letters were shown to a member of parliament who shared Le Caron's father's concern and who suggested that the British government be informed. Such was the political climate at the time that the matter was soon brought to the attention of the Home Secretary who, detecting a new Irish menace across the Atlantic, asked for a detailed report from Le Caron on what he had learned about the Fenians. Flattered, Le Caron complied. He did not know much, but he told what he knew.

The Harley Street Recruit

The Irish invasion of Canada, in which about 500 Fenians participated, started June 1, 1866 and ended in disarray the following day. Le Caron's information had not been of much help. It had not been specific on either date or place and the Canadians were taken by surprise. However, they soon rallied and easily outnumbered and overwhelmed the attackers, 60 of whom were killed. Another 200 were captured. Most of the rest retreated back to the United States across the Niagara River in flatboats, to be taken briefly into custody by the American authorities. The Fenians never had a chance of success but, in British eyes, Le Caron emerged from the escapade as a source of potentially valuable information.

When he visited England to see his parents soon afterwards, he was led to believe that he would be summoned by government officials in London to report on whatever else he might have learned about Irish-American political-military developments. Though he had little to add to what he had already said, the prospect of such a consultation pleased him. He was even more pleased when, instead of merely being called in for a friendly chat, he was asked, in confidence, to come to an innocent-looking house in London's Harley Street and was formally recruited into the British secret service.

Le Caron's old army friend, John O'Neill, had shortly before become president of the Fenian Brotherhood in the United States and Le Caron was asked to penetrate the Brotherhood on behalf of British intelligence. He unhesitatingly agreed. Totally accidental circumstances, coinciding with Le Caron's sudden feelings of pride in his English origins, had conspired to create a spy.

Back in America, the Fenians, seeking to recover from their Canadian fiasco, were busily revamping their military arm, which badly needed reorganization and strengthening. A recruit like Major Le Caron, a man with proven military experience, was warmly welcomed to the ranks. Few questions were asked about the Irish ancestry his mother suddenly acquired to justify the allegiance of this American former army officer of supposed French origins.

Many of the key Fenian military positions were already filled so Le Caron volunteered to go to Illinois, where he had already established a home after the Civil War, and where he would organize Fenian groups among the growing number of Irish-Americans there, while proceeding with his medical studies. Through his friendship with O'Neill, he developed a reputation among the Fenians as a military expert and was called upon repeatedly for advice concerning the rebuilding of the Fenian military structure and, specifically, about preparations for the next invasion of Canada. There were men to train, supplies to acquire and store, and strategic decisions to make. Le Caron's position, especially after he was appointed Fenian inspector-general, gave him access to much information, which he transmitted to British intelligence. So high was his standing in the Brotherhood that Le Caron was included in the delegation that visited American President

Andrew Johnson to hear of his sympathy for the cause of an independent Ireland, an unpublicized declaration of which the British government was soon informed.

Perhaps the most extraordinary aspect of Le Caron's adventures was how limited was his initial understanding of espionage methods. His success was due more to Fenian neglect of security than to his own talents. His spying career almost came to an early end when, meeting a high-ranking Fenian official for the first time, he questioned him closely about other leading Fenians and recorded their names, in the presence of his informant, with such meticulousness that suspicion was aroused. It was overcome only through the intercession of other, less suspicious Fenian officials.

Also remarkable was how little Le Caron knew about the background of the object of his espionage efforts, the situation in Ireland and Irish grievances. Called upon to make speeches at Irish-American gatherings, he lived in dread of being compelled to make specific references. He managed to get by with generalizations about the glories of Irish culture, the bestiality of English repression and the spirit of patriotism which motivated his audiences. Modern counter-espionage methods would have chopped down this proud, resourceful amateur very early in the game.

But Le Caron thrived in the Irish-American arena he had penetrated. Not only was he appointed to a senior position in the more militant *Clan na Gael* secret organization when it was formed following Fenian failures to which he had contributed, but he was also dispatched as an emissary between Irish-American secret groups and Irish leaders in London and Paris. As always, British intelligence was kept fully informed. As for his private life, growing Irish influence in local American politics gained for Le Caron considerable patronage in American cities with influential Irish population.

Having completed his medical studies and having become a doctor, he gained easy access to various official medical boards and organizations and became a respected medical administrator.

Through the information Le Caron had provided, the Canadians had been better prepared for the second Fenian assault in 1870, which was easily brushed off. But that defeat, and others, aroused deep frustration among many Irish-Americans. This ultimately found expression in plans for the dispatch of men to dynamite targets in London, including parliament, the Tower of London, railway stations and bridges. Some of the attacks were foiled by independent British police action; others as a result of information Le Caron was able to pass on. But some of the dynamiters got through and the resulting explosions provoked a panic atmosphere in London.

The British authorities decided that special action was required to reassure the public about security measures and thus defuse some of the tension. Le Caron was summoned home to England to testify about Irish-American conspiracies. He made dramatic public appearances in London, during which he revealed much about Irish revolutionaries, exaggerating shamelessly but helping instil the impression that everything was under control. The 20-year-long career of the spy by accident had come to an end.

Irish Prospects

Just as British intelligence used Le Caron against Irish revolutionaries, so, over the years, several other countries have sought to exploit anti-British Irish militants for their own purposes. Napoleon, seeking to conquer Britain, was tempted by advocates of Irish independence to land troops there and free Ireland from British rule. After examining the prospects, the French Emperor decided it was not a viable operation.

During the First World War, Germany, through the

instrument of its secret service, sent arms to assist in the 1916 rising in Dublin against British rule, but the arms were intercepted. The desire to undermine British capitalism aroused Russian interest in backing the underground Irish Republican Army in the 1930s. But Moscow's plans to assist the IRA foundered when Soviet intelligence liaison agents reported that the Irish revolutionaries were too undisciplined, unpredictable and insubordinate — in short, that they could not be relied upon to take orders.

During the Second World War, Nazi Germany tried to exploit the IRA to expose Britain's otherwise secure rear and weaken its war effort. However, the Irish government and people were too anti-Nazi, and the IRA too disorganized, for the operation to make any meaningful headway.

Since the Second World War, the KGB has maintained contact with the IRA through its agents in the recently established Soviet Embassy in Dublin and in Russian news agencies. It has arranged for the supply of small arms to the Irish revolutionaries for use in Northern Ireland, a shipment of which (Czechoslovak-made weapons) was intercepted in the Netherlands in 1972. The KGB has, however, maintained a very low profile, partly because it still considers the IRA too undisciplined, partly because it frowns upon support for the IRA from the strongly anti-Communist Irish-American community, and partly because the Russians do not think possible rewards for Moscow in the Ulster problem are worth a diplomatic incident with Britain.

Nevertheless, Moscow is aware of and appreciates the fact that the trouble in Northern Ireland (which remains part of the United Kingdom) could weaken British defences in the event of an intensification of the Cold War and that the Ulster situation has compelled Britain to reduce the forces available for duty on the North Atlantic Treaty Organization front line in West Germany.

4. Spymaster Turned Around

There is nothing new about people being blackmailed because of their sexual deviations. Nor is it restricted to espionage. But probably the most far-reaching consequences of sexual blackmail sprang from a complicated spy drama in central Europe just before the First World War, an episode that hastened the collapse of the Austrian Empire. The chief participants were the Russian intelligence service and Colonel Alfred Redl, a respected Austrian general staff officer with a secret fondness for boys and young men.

The son of a minor railway official, Redl had risen remarkably quickly through the ranks of the Austrian Army, whose ossified officer corps did not often welcome among its members individuals of such modest origins. But while still a young man, Redl displayed military talents, a sharpness of mind, great dignity and surface propriety which overcame upper class prejudice. By the time he was forty years old, he had become deputy director and dominant personality in the *Kundschaftsstelle,* the Austrian military intelligence agency.

His performance won him widespread respect, admiration and confidence. He compiled a detailed stylebook for espionage operations, probably the first ever. It outlined what seemed at the time every move a good spy or counter-spy should make in every conceivable circumstance. He introduced the use of photography as a matter of routine in counter-espionage, having all persons who visited his office photographed by hidden cameras. His was the first use of bugging devices; primitive recordings were made of conversations in his office. Redl's superiors considered him a genius.

When he was promoted to the position of chief-of-staff of an Austrian army corps, his successor (and former protégé) in the intelligence service, Major Maximillian Ronge, felt obliged to emerge from Redl's shadow through innovations of his own. One of those innovations, more methodical postal control, was to be Alfred Redl's downfall.

Redl had been driven to treason early in his career, when it became apparent that he was destined for high rank. Not only was his homosexuality something the Austrian High Command would never have tolerated, but his penchant for luxurious living had resulted in irredeemably huge debts. Russian intelligence monitored his secret behaviour for several years before springing the trap. Redl was approached in Vienna and, at a rendezvous arranged in the Vienna Woods, was told that his secrets were known and might be exposed. The alternative, if he cooperated, was more than enough money to wipe out his debts, and not a word to anyone about his unconventional personal inclinations.

Redl succumbed and became one of the most extraordinary double agents in history. His entry into service for Russian intelligence did not, however, diminish his enthusiasm for improving the techniques of the Austrian intelligence service. The security methods he introduced, the rigorous training of Austrian agents, his success in impressing generals with the importance of the proper use of intelligence, gained him ever-increasing admiration, even in the Imperial Court in Vienna. At the same time, he was transmitting to the Russians whatever secrets he could lay his hands on about the Austrian army's strategic plans and about his country's fortifications. He sent Moscow details of the identity, whereabouts and missions of Austrian secret agents in Russia, some of whom he had himself dispatched. Where possible, he prevented Russian secrets which nevertheless fell into Austrian hands from reaching his superiors; when those secrets got through anyway, he made certain they were not considered important.

Russian turncoats who offered to sell secrets to Austria were brought to him and, before transactions could be completed, the would-be informants mysteriously disappeared.

Redl's services were so appreciated by the Russians that even after he was promoted from his job in intelligence, and the range of Austrian secrets accessible to him was greatly restricted, they continued to send him money with which to maintain his extravagant living standards. He owned houses in Prague and Vienna, an estate in the Austrian countryside, several cars, expensive works of art and a superb wine cellar.

The End for Redl

The money he received from the Russians was dispatched to him at regular intervals, addressed to a fictitious person in care of a post box at Vienna's central post office in the heart of the old city. One day, in accordance with Major Ronge's new dedication to postal surveillance, two bulky envelopes, which arrived at the post office from a border town known to be an active centre of Russian espionage, were intercepted and opened by Austrian intelligence officers. They were found to contain substantial sums of money.

Ronge was immediately informed and knew he had stumbled across something worth watching. Arrangements were made for the clerk at the post box section of the post office to press a buzzer connected to an alarm in an office in the police station next door when someone showed up to claim the suspicious envelopes. Two detectives were assigned to wait for the signal and to pounce on the recipient.

Almost three months went by before the buzzer sounded. The detectives were not in the office at the police station at the time. By the time they were found and raced to the post office, the man who had called for the envelopes had taken them and made off in a taxi. While the detectives deliberated in the street on how to explain to Ronge what had happened, a taxi drew up in front of them and, remarkably, turned out to be the same one the mysterious stranger had taken and which had driven him to a cafe not far away. At a taxi rank in front of the cafe, they learned that the man they were looking for might have been the same one who had taken another taxi to a hotel across town.

The lobby staff at the hotel could not help them — too many people came and went all the time. But the reception clerk was given a knife sheath which the detectives had found on the passenger seat of the taxi the suspect had taken from the post office (Redl had used the knife to open his money-laden envelopes) and was asked to try to discover if it belonged to any of the hotel guests. Later that day, the waiting detectives recognized the famous Colonel Alfred Redl when he accepted the sheath as his own and thanked the reception clerk for finding it.

The detectives were astonished. It was possible, they thought, that, though no longer in intelligence, Redl was involved in a secret mission on behalf of the Austrian general staff. But so close had they come to disgrace at the post office that they hastened to report on what they had discovered. From then on, it was only a matter of some detailed detective work, overcoming the shocked incredulity of Redl's fellow senior officers, and closing in.

Redl himself was soon aware that he was being observed and followed. He made half-hearted attempts to throw off his 'shadows', but no serious effort to escape. The end came for him in true romantic style, so characteristic of so much that happened in central Europe during the last years of the Austrian Empire. He was visited at his hotel in Vienna by four senior army officers. They confronted him with the suspicions, now largely confirmed, which he had aroused. Redl received them graciously and said everything they wished to know could be found at his home in Prague. He then borrowed a revolver from one of the officers, all of whom courteously withdrew. Early the following morning, a detective, who respectfully had remained downstairs in the lobby through the night, went to Redl's room to make certain the revolver had been used. He then left discreetly, called the hotel from outside and asked to be put through to Redl. Knowing him to be in but getting no reply, the hotel investigated.

It was made to look like a suicide, committed for unknown personal reasons. However, efforts to conceal the facts and prevent a scandal were frustrated by press leaks on the immense extent of Redl's treason, disclosed when his Prague home was examined. Among other things, documents found there made it clear that the Russians had acquired from him the Austrian military code and had been able to intercept and decipher all Austrian military secrets transmitted by radio. It was possible that the Russians had also received details of Austria's basic military strategy and primary tactics for the war that most people realized was about to erupt, as indeed it did a few months later.

Changes were hastily improvised. But flexibility had never been a characteristic of the Austrian military mind. When the war broke out, the smaller Serbian army, supplied by the Russians with secrets Redl had passed on, was able to cut the Austrians to pieces. The four-century-old Austrian Empire had been succumbing to the ravages of time and history even before the war. It could not survive the defeat to which Redl had made a small but significant contribution. It crumbled and vanished from the scene before peace returned to Europe again.

5. *The Prodigy*

Spymasters generally work from afar, manipulating their networks from secure rear bases, usually in their own countries. If their presence is required at the scene of an espionage operation, they are likely to appear under an inviolable cloak of diplomatic immunity, assured of an easy exit should problems arise. Such, however, was not the case for Richard Sorge, the German who became a Soviet spymaster and the most successful Russian spy of all time, the man who, it can credibly be argued, saved Moscow from capture by invading armies from his own country.

A *Hero of the Soviet Union* (the award was made posthumously), Sorge's achievements were sufficiently monumental to make him, though a foreigner, the first Soviet secret agent publicly acclaimed by the Russians. General Douglas MacArthur, the post-Second World War American commander in occupied Japan, Sorge's old stamping ground, called his achievements 'a brilliant success in espionage'. And MacArthur did not normally lavish praise on Communists.

Sorge was born (1895) in Russia and his mother was Russian. But his father was a German, an engineer temporarily employed in Russia at the time of Sorge's birth. Sorge was taken to Germany while still an infant and brought up there. He felt so strongly about his German nationality that he enlisted in the German army when the First World War erupted and, despite serious wounds he sustained as an infantryman, volunteered for further combat duty and was wounded again.

After the war, revolutionaries tried to exploit the chaos prevailing in defeated, demoralized Germany to bring about a Communist revolution. They failed to do so, but succeeded in winning many new recruits to their banners, including Richard Sorge. Like many of his contemporaries, Sorge hoped a new social order could be constructed to rescue Germany, and the world, from the perils of unemployment, hunger and national conflict. It was, and is, a recurring theme — the underlying motivation for many idealistic, disappointed or frustrated individuals who turn to extremist political movements for personal salvation and the salvation of the world.

Sorge brought to his new loyalty the same energy and zeal with which he had served as a soldier. By the time he joined the Communists, he had completed university studies in political science, had worked briefly as a coal miner to learn what it was like to be a proletarian, and had established rudimentary credentials as a journalist. His diligence and dedication soon attracted the attention of Soviet agents active in Germany at the time. Sorge was summoned to Moscow where he was recruited by the GRU (Soviet military intelligence) and instructed to break all ties he had made with his Communist comrades in Germany.

After three years of intensive espionage training in Russia, Sorge was sent out on intelligence gathering exercises abroad to California, Scandinavia and Britain, where Scotland Yard's Special Branch, examining its files, uncovered his Communist background in Germany, suspected he was a spy and had him expelled. Despite this misadventure, Sorge was considered by his Soviet superiors to be a promising agent, ready for his first major assignment. He was dispatched to Shanghai to set up a Soviet spy ring in China.

Setting about this task with considerable resourcefulness, he rapidly mastered the complexities of the unsettled and confusing Chinese situation and recruited and stationed agents in key cities. But, exercising an independence of imagination not commonly exhibited by Soviet agents, Sorge became quickly convinced that he was wasting his time. He believed that China's internal disunity and basic weakness made it largely irrelevant in terms of Russian national interests. He informed Moscow that the real potential threat was Japan and ultimately was able to persuade his superiors to transfer him to

Tokyo where he arrived in 1934.

Before leaving for Japan, Sorge, remembering his expulsion from Britain years earlier, took steps to cover his tracks. He settled briefly in Berlin where he joined the Nazi Party and the Nazi press club. He also arranged to represent several German publications, including a prominent Frankfurt newspaper, when he got to Tokyo. This eminently wise precaution contained its own dangers. The Stalin purges in Russia were gathering momentum and the personnel of Soviet espionage agencies were not exempt from the irrational direction and intensity they developed. Absolute loyalty was no protection. Soon many of Stalin's earliest comrades would be absurdly confessing to having been traitors all along. Both of Sorge's predecessors as chief Russian secret agent in Tokyo were to be executed in the purges and Vyacheslav Menzhinsky, the head of Soviet intelligence, died in Russia under mysterious circumstances at about the time Sorge was launching his operations in Japan. Nazi affiliations, even if only contrived for operational purposes, exposed him to the kind of senseless suspicion, accusations and condemnations which were beginning to cast a shroud over Russia and claim the lives of an untold number of its people.

But Sorge was convinced that the risk he took was essential to establish adequate cover in Tokyo. He was fortunate to have been an agent of the GRU rather than the NKVD (a KGB antecedent). Developments within the GRU, during even the worst of the purge period, tended to be less hysterical than in other Soviet official agencies.

Sorge had already begun establishing the core of his Japan network before he left China. Once established in Tokyo, he proceeded methodically to put everything in place. Among his key agents was Ozaki Hozumi, a brilliant journalist with contacts in the sacrosanct imperial family and, through it, with the Japanese government. At one point, Ozaki was made a Japanese government adviser on Chinese affairs, giving him wide access to confidential information. Another of Sorge's key men was Max Klausen, a German ex-seaman who transmitted Sorge's messages to Moscow from a fishing boat to escape detection by the Japanese security police.

By the time Sorge had finished constructing his network, it consisted of dozens of agents, including officials and lesser ranking personnel in various government ministries and agencies, journalists, and others in positions to acquire secret information of use to the Soviet Union as the clouds of war spread across the world. The information covered a wide range of subjects — military hardware, military deployment and planning, and diplomatic and economic developments. Unlike most Soviet agents, Sorge did not confine himself merely to transmitting what he learned. He tied things together and analysed the results, offering Moscow a comprehensive picture of what was happening in Japan, a more precise and substantial interpretation than the Russians could have expected from their home-bred analysts.

Sorge himself acquired some of the more important individual items of intelligence. He had become friendly with Eugen Ott, the German ambassador in Tokyo, who believed that Sorge was what he pretended to be — an ardent Nazi. He often breakfasted with Ott, offering the ambassador titillating bits of gossip about officials and official life in Tokyo, in return for which Ott, innocently and casually, provided Sorge with details of German-Japanese relations and Japanese military plans of which he, as ambassador of Japan's main European ally, was kept informed. So well did they get on, that Ott appointed Sorge press attaché at the German embassy, which put him in a position to learn even more.

Sorge was able to warn Moscow in advance about the

German invasion of Poland in 1939 and of German armies massing for the invasion of Russia in 1941. Much of the information was ignored by Stalin and the Russian High Command who were, by then, inundated by reports, many of them false, from agents all over the world, and reeling under the impact of the realization of how weak the Russian armed forces were, compared to those of the Germans.

But one vital secret passed on by Sorge was taken seriously and acted upon, with the result that the German invasion of Russia was forced to grind to a halt, and was then thrown back, earlier than it otherwise would have been. Millions of Russian lives were probably saved. With the German armies advancing relentlessly on Moscow, Sorge was able to report that the Japanese had, after careful consideration, decided not to attack Russia, but to concentrate on driving the British out of Southeast Asia and the Americans out of the Pacific. Relieved, the Russians were able to shift large numbers of troops and large quantities of weapons from their eastern borders to take the brunt of the German *blitzkrieg* and ultimately to send the German armies reeling back towards Berlin and defeat.

The Japanese knew, well before Sorge was finally apprehended in 1941, that a major foreign espionage ring was operating out of Tokyo, probably with an agent well-placed in the crowded German embassy. But, though they kept Sorge and most foreign residents under surveillance, they had been unable to crack the network. Sorge usually made contact with his agents under the cover of loud, orgiastic parties at his home, an indulgence many in the foreign community practised. Suspicion began to fall on Sorge when one of his minor agents, a Japanese, was arrested for suspected Communist activity and, to save himself, implicated other secret Communists. Some of these, it was discovered, frequented Sorge's loud parties.

But Sorge's end, which was probably inevitable by then, resulted directly from one of the few security lapses he had ever permitted himself. Though a ladies' man (he was handsome, charming and attractive to females), he had always been careful to keep his personal behaviour from jeopardizing his espionage activities. It remains a mystery why, when he knew Japanese counter-intelligence was being intensified, he took up with a new girlfriend who, he should have suspected, was a Japanese counter-espionage agent assigned to discover whether Sorge was as innocent as he seemed.

Almost immediately, the girl recognized that he warranted close surveillance. She saw him receive a secret message in a rolled-up ball of rice paper from a restaurant waiter. The next time she saw such a message passed, she managed to alert Japanese security which recovered it after Sorge had negligently thrown it away. Both messages were warnings that counterintelligence was closing in. The warnings had come too late. Sorge was arrested just before he could pass on to Moscow the news that Japan planned to bomb Pearl Harbour early in December, 1941 and bring America into the war. (It remains debateable whether the Russians, who wanted America in, would have passed the message on to Washington had they received it.) Sorge was hanged in Tokyo in 1944.

Until recently, the Soviet Union was not in the habit of paying public tribute to its spies. A country which incessantly warns its people that enemy spies are lurking everywhere is not likely to draw attention to the fact that it deploys secret agents as well. But the great debt Russia owed its man in Tokyo changed all that -- if belatedly. There is now a street in Moscow named after Richard Sorge and a ship in the Soviet merchant fleet bears his name.

6. The Moscow Leak

On October 22, 1962, at the height of the Cold War between America and Russia, the President of the United States made a calculated decision that was widely interpreted as risking nuclear holocaust. President John Kennedy ordered the American navy to intercept and inspect Soviet merchant ships en route to Cuba. If the ships carried nuclear weapons or missile launching equipment, they were to be unceremoniously turned back and prevented from reaching their planned destination.

'Intolerable piracy,' the Russians called it and, indeed, it would have been difficult to construct a persuasive strictly legal case in defence of the American peacetime 'quarantine'. Nevertheless, Kennedy was convinced of the propriety of his actions. He had been shown photographic evidence that the Russians were busily engaged in constructing secret missile installations in Cuba, a mere 90 miles from the southeast tip of the United States. The threat to American security was so great that Kennedy believed he was preventing a nuclear war rather than risking one by ordering Russian missile-transporting cargo vessels to be turned away.

The fact that the Russians knuckled under when confronted with the American challenge and humiliatingly withdrew missile launching equipment they had, in fact, been assembling in Cuba seemed to justify Kennedy's dangerous move. Nevertheless, instead of meekly climbing down, the Russians might well have replied with a nuclear attack and all-out war and many people questioned whether Kennedy had the right to play global poker with so much at stake.

But, while it is impossible to predict how so proud and powerful a nation as the Soviet Union will respond to being publicly humbled, American intelligence had a reasonably good idea of the limited strategic options open to the Russians.

The Russians were, in fact, in no position to challenge the far-flung might of America's military forces, which had already been put on the alert. Kennedy was aware of this when he ordered the American navy to stop Russian ships on the high seas.

During the previous 16 months, Oleg Penkovsky, a high-ranking Soviet military intelligence officer, had supplied western intelligence with a large, up-to-date catalogue of Soviet military secrets, including those concerned with missile strength and deployment. Penkovsky had also conveyed a vivid impression of the likely attitude of Russian military strategists to possible nuclear confrontation with the United States. This information contributed to Russia's most serious single Cold War setback and a total reappraisal in Moscow of Russia's worldwide military strategy.

The secrets Penkovsky transmitted to the West were not restricted to missiles. They included details of developments in Soviet aircraft, armoured weapons and other tools of war. They included information on the deployment and mission of Soviet forces in Eastern Europe and in Asia. They included the names and assignments of many Soviet intelligence agents (most of them cloaked by diplomatic immunity) in western and other countries.

It is likely that Penkovsky gave the West advance notice of Soviet permission for East Germany to construct the notorious Berlin Wall, enabling the West to prepare its response to this violation of treaties. (Although the Wall was vigorously condemned by the West, many believed that, without it, the exodus of East Germans to West Germany, and the higher living standards and personal freedoms there, would have so threatened East Germany with lasting impoverishment that a new war in central Europe might have been difficult to avoid. After some months of apparently dangerous East-West confrontation over the Wall, the situation in central Europe calmed considerably.)

Background

By the time Penkovsky was arrested in Moscow, at the height of the Cuba missiles crisis, he had become the most valuable western agent ever to have penetrated Soviet officialdom. His credentials within the Russian military establishment were impeccable. A graduate of the Kiev artillery school, he had served with distinction in the Second World War, earning 13 military decorations. After the war, he attended the Frunze Military Academy, the equivalent of America's West Point and Britain's Sandhurst. Many of his fellow cadets were later to fill important military posts and, innocently, were to provide him with information and informed opinions which were duly passed on to the West.

After the Frunze Academy, Penkovsky was channelled into intelligence work. He was sent for training at the Military Diplomatic Academy after which he was assigned to the GRU (Soviet military intelligence). By then, he numbered among his friends such important personages as Marshal Sergei Varentsov, who was in charge of Soviet tactical missile forces, and General Ivan Serov, chief of military intelligence. His father-in-law was a rocket warfare expert with high military and Communist Party connections, and his great uncle, General Valentin Penkovsky, was commander of Soviet forces deployed in the Far East.

Nevertheless, his first assignment abroad almost led to an end to Penkovsky's career in intelligence work. Differences with his superior officer over what Penkovsky considered inefficient procedure resulted in his recall to Moscow and a severe reprimand. But, with the help of his connections, the incident was made to work to his advantage, confirming his dedication to duty on behalf of his homeland. After a brief spell in bureaucratic limbo in Moscow, he was sent to missile school and then assigned to — and soon became deputy chief of — the Soviet Scientific Research Committee. The committee's function was to deal with foreign businessmen and scientists for purposes of trade and exchange of information between Russia and other countries. An important part of its job, and the focus of interest of the GRU officers who ran it, was to recruit agents from among the foreigners with whom it dealt, to gather secret information from them, and to cope with situations in which the foreign visitors were actually on spying missions directed against Soviet interests.

Penkovsky's decision to spy for the West was slow to build. For years, he had nourished resentment against the Soviet system. He was appalled by the attitudes and standards of the Soviet upper classes, particularly the military elite. He believed its members were primarily motivated by personal ambition and greed and he had observed many of them intriguing against one another for promotion. Though a Communist Party member since his youth, Penkovsky had also come to believe that Communism was a fraud, criminally harmful to both Russia and the Russian people. He was convinced that Premier Nikita Khrushchev was preparing to launch a new world war to extend the Kremlin's power.

In most classic cases of recruitment of spies abroad, the initiative comes from the intelligence organization that is to benefit from the acquisition of secret information. But the Penkovsky case was different. His growing contempt for Soviet leaders and the Soviet system led him to make the approach, first to the Americans who spurned him, fearing he was a KGB *provocateur,* and then to the British who decided he was genuine and who cultivated him on behalf of themselves and the Americans.

His tenure as a working spy was not long. But from early

1961 until late 1962, he passed on to the West thousands of photographs of classified Soviet military documents. He visited London twice and Paris once, during which he conferred with British and American intelligence officers to convey information personally and to receive instructions and equipment (miniature cameras and coding devices) to continue and intensify his espionage work back in Moscow.

Much of his information was transmitted to the West through travelling British businessman and secret agent Greville Wynne, who was arrested in Hungary by the Russians in November, 1962 while en route to Russia to try to smuggle Penkovsky out of the West after it had become clear his days in Moscow were numbered. (Penkovsky had, in fact, already been arrested.) Both Wynne and Penkovsky stood trial in Moscow in 1963. Wynne was jailed and later exchanged for Russian spy Konon Molody, who had been imprisoned in Britain. Penkovsky was executed.

The Soviet authorities sought to conceal the fact that Penkovsky had had access to important information or that the secrets he had transmitted to the West were of great significance. However, a different impression is given by a number of developments which followed hard on the heels of Penkovsky's arrest. The marshal in charge of Soviet missile installations was dismissed. There was a thorough shake-up of Soviet military intelligence, with its director relieved of his command. More than 200 Soviet agents, most of them diplomats, were hurriedly summoned home from various parts of the world and reassigned to domestic posts. Penkovsky's actions had bitten hard and they had bitten deep.

7. The Spy Above Suspicion

At the high point of his remarkable career, Russian spy Harold Adrian Russell Philby was on his way towards accomplishing an unprecedented act of espionage. Though there were other candidates as well, he might have ended up as top man in an adversary intelligence service, Britain's MI 6, a post he would have filled as a secret enemy agent.

'Kim' Philby had all the qualifications for heading British intelligence — a seemingly distinguished career and meteoric rise in Britain's espionage apparatus, the required public school and university background, the right connections, a skill for bureaucratic infighting, as well as intelligence, diligence and charm.

Nevertheless, this pillar of the British establishment, destined for high office, had been a Russian agent virtually all his adult life. In that capacity, he devastatingly undermined Britain's intelligence services and caused the death or imprisonment of hundreds of western agents and anti-Communist rebels. He turned his back on his origins and upbringing — and all the substantial rewards they offered — to become a secret renegade of monumental proportions.

Philby had inherited a contempt for conventional authority and behaviour from his father. The elder Philby, one of the most distinguished arabists of his generation, became a Moslem, took the name Abdullah (his real name was Harry St. John Philby) and spent much of his later life in Arabia, disappearing periodically into the desert wastelands dressed as an Arab. He was headstrong and opinionated; his forcefulness may have been at least partly responsible for Kim Philby's lifelong stammer and generally introverted nature, both of which probably directed his rebellion along a clandestine rather than a conspicuous path.

But whatever influence his father's character may have had, the personal mutiny which Kim Philby chose to mount was very much a product of his own times. The early 1930s, when he attended Cambridge University, were years of depression, of widespread poverty and unemployment. Like many of his contemporaries, Philby found Communism a potent attraction, offering both a body of dogma to substitute for religion and a dynamic programme of social action. Some converts remained Communists the rest of their lives. But for many, it was a temporary commitment, terminated by the shock of the Soviet-Nazi Friendship Pact of 1939. Others retained the faith until disillusioned by Russian imperialism in Eastern Europe after the Second World War or by the crimes which Joseph Stalin perpetrated against his own people, irrefutably documented by Stalin's successor, Nikita Khrushchev.

However, Philby's conversion to Communism was total and enduring, so complete that — like his father — he took on a disguise to serve his new faith. While other young Englishmen of similar persuasion enrolled in Communist organizations and vigorously espoused the Communist cause in public, Philby did the opposite. Acting under instructions from Soviet intelligence, he went into ideological hiding. He meticulously constructed an artificial facade that was to mask his true allegiance for almost thirty years.

At first, Philby made no secret of his political inclinations. He became a Communist during his last year at Cambridge and, after leaving university, went to Austria where he openly identified with local Communists. Indeed, he married an Austrian Communist, Litzi Kohlmann. It was, however, a brief venture into the realm of candid, undisguised behaviour. Philby was about to retreat into the shadows.

In 1934, at the age of 23, he returned to England and proceeded to distance himself from the surface trappings of his ideological commitment. He methodically cut himself off from his leftist friends. By mutual agreement, he and his wife quietly separated — divorce might have attracted attention to the fact that he had married a Communist. He joined the Nazi-dominated Anglo-German Fellowship.

A 'sleeper' was in the making. Philby was being carefully groomed for future use by his Soviet control, though, at that stage, no one in Moscow could have foreseen how rich a vein was being tapped.

At the time, *The Times* of London was widely and justifiably known as an organ of the British establishment, its every word gospel, its every contributor a man of probity and distinction. There were few better routes to immediate acceptance by the establishment than through *The Times*. After consulting with Russian intelligence, Philby set out to follow that path. It was not an easy objective. Jobs were hard to come by in the mid-thirties. Though some junior executives and other personnel of the newspaper were old school mates of his, a frontal assault on the old headquarters of *The Times,* at London's Printing House Square, seemed inadvisable. Philby resorted to more subtle tactics.

He set off for Spain as a free-lance journalist to cover the Spanish Civil War. Shunning the loyalist side, which was supported by the Communists, he made for the front lines manned by the nationalist forces of General Franco, which had the sympathies of the editor of *The Times* as well as the Nazis. Once established there, Philby began dispatching unsolicited articles back to London, well-written and containing no more than a slight pro-nationalist bias, enough to permit those favouring Franco to claim they were objective while proving that Franco was both right and winning. *The Times* soon began printing the occasional Philby article and, after one of them lent credence to the false claim that the loyalist forces themselves, rather than Franco's forces, had destroyed the town of Guernica, Philby was named *Times* special correspondent in Spain. His climb up the ladder had begun.

Any lingering questions about his earlier Communist

allegiance were overcome when General Franco personally conferred on Philby a medal of Military Merit for his services.In 1939, with the Second World War imminent, *The Times* transferred him to France, from which he was evacuated with British forces the following year.

Objective in Sight

British intelligence services had been badly neglected between the world wars. With the onset of hostilities, they expanded rapidly. But experienced intelligence officers were in short supply. In view of his work for *The Times* in Spain, his public school background and the establishment connections that were now his, Philby was a natural recruit. His assignment was to train agents for undercover assignments in Europe, a job for which he soon developed a reputation as an expert. It was widely suspected that he had been a British secret agent during his time in Spain, and very few British officers knew anything at all at the time about training secret agents. An intelligent, quiet, efficient man, Philby did nothing to disabuse anyone of illusions about his expertise. He got on with the job, improvising where necessary; everyone was new to the operation and few meaningful guidelines had been laid down.

His performance was so effective that within a year, Philby was transferred from teaching to planning espionage operations, a major coup for the Russians who now had a man on the road to total penetration of British intelligence.

The significance of this development was limited during the Second World War, when both British and Soviet intelligence concentrated on defeating their mutual German enemy. But Philby was able to offer Moscow a description of the kind of underground organization the British were striving to construct in German-occupied Eastern Europe, information that was to prove useful when the Russians replaced the

Germans as over-lords of the area. He was also able to intercept and divert some of the reports to Britain of growing opposition to Hitler within the German army. Russia's paranoiac hierarchy feared that an anti-Soviet alliance might be forged between the Germans, on the brink of defeat, and the conquering Western Allies.

But this period remained essentially a preparatory stage for Philby's progress towards the centre of British intelligence. As the war drew to a close, however, he was assigned to head a new British espionage bureau, established to operate against the Russians, and against Communist espionage in general. This appointment was more than the Russians could ever have hoped to gain from a British 'sleeper'. Aside from obvious benefits to be derived by the Russians from having their own man direct British anti-Russian operations, there would be few espionage secrets in British hands to which Philby (and the KGB) would not have access.

However, Philby's career almost ended in disaster in 1945 when a Russian diplomat he gave his name as Volkov — turned up at the British embassy in Istanbul, asked for political asylum, and offered a sample of the information he was prepared to give in exchange. It included the claim that the KGB had planted a man in British counter-espionage. Volkov was told that instructions on his request for asylum had to come from London, and come they did, in the form of a badly frightened Kim Philby who had arranged to have himself dispatched to Istanbul to investigate on behalf of the British authorities. Not surprisingly, Volkov was no longer to be found. Some days later, a man with a bandaged face was carried on a stretcher to a waiting Soviet military plane at Istanbul Airport and flown to Russia. Volkov and the secrets he had to offer the West, possibly implicating Philby, were never heard of again.

Philby also managed to escape suspicion when, while stationed in Washington in 1949, he was British organizer of a joint Anglo-American campaign to infiltrate Albanian refugees back into Albania to start an anti-Communist uprising. Moscow was kept informed and wherever the Albanian rebels landed in their homeland, Communist security forces were waiting. Hundreds were executed.

Philby's rise within the British intelligence establishment was inexorable, despite the fact that things were going wrong. The Russians unmistakably were doing better than might have been expected in coping with British secret operations. British agents active in Communist countries were being apprehended far too frequently. There had to be a spy well placed in British ranks. But Philby, modest, efficient, well-connected, the charming stammerer, was above suspicion. As link man between British and American intelligence, he continued to gain access to an ever wider range of secret information — though the Americans, badly stung by the recent loss of atom secrets to the Russians, were increasingly cautious about everyone and everything. Washington was the wrong place for Philby to make his one known serious blunder.

He had learned in 1951 that British counter-espionage was zeroing on British diplomat, Donald MacLean, who was also a Russian spy. Philby not only sent a warning to MacLean through Foreign Office man Anthony Burgess, who was serving the Russians as well, but he permitted Burgess, who was already under American suspicion, to stay at his Washington home before returning to London to tip off MacLean. It was a foolish, needless risk to take. When both MacLean and Burgess subsequently fled to Russia, the accusing finger inevitably pointed at Philby.

Furious by now at the amount of secret information known to have been channelled to the Russians, and considering

British intelligence a sieve, the Americans would have nothing more to do with him and he was hastily shipped back to London for a departmental investigation. Though he was dismissed from government service after a searching but inconclusive inquiry, Philby's success in covering his tracks and establishment reputation saved him from exposure as a Russian spy at that point.

He scrounged a living in journalism and related fields in London during the next few years. In 1956, British intelligence helped him line up freelance assignments in the Middle East from two reputable British journals. Enough information had been unearthed by then to indicate that he had been working for the Russians. It was hoped that he could be used to ensnare Russian agents into a British counter-espionage trap, so that the Philby affair would not amount to a complete loss. But nothing came of it. Tiring of the charade, or expecting imminent arrest, or possibly fearing execution by the CIA, Philby disappeared in Beirut one night in 1963 and turned up in Moscow several weeks later, announcing, 'I have come home'.

8. The Big Switch

There is nothing unique about a turned spy. Many an espionage agent, to save his life when 'blown' or when tempted by money or other inducements, has switched sides. But Reinhard Gehlen has the distinction of being the only spymaster in history who ran an extensive espionage service for one country and then put it at the disposal of another. The chief of Germany's Second World War intelligence bureau directed against the Soviet Union and Eastern Europe, Gehlen transferred his allegiance, and what he could salvage of his apparatus, to the United States when Germany was defeated by the United States and its wartime allies.

Born in 1902, Gehlen grew to maturity between the two

world wars, when social upheaval and economic chaos in Germany made a mockery of the concepts of order and solidity which marked his Prussian upbringing. Through family tradition and reaching for an island of stability in the turbulent sea of inter-war uncertainty, he enrolled in the German Army at the age of 18. At the time, the German Army was sharply restricted in size and activity by the Versailles Treaty imposed by the victorious allies at the close of the First World War. Though he soon graduated from officers' training school, there was little room for advancement for even so diligent an officer as Reinhard Gehlen, who combined the soldierly virtues of personal austerity and strategic imagination with the intellect of a scholar.

But the Nazi rise to power in 1933 led to a regeneration of German military forces with which Hitler intended to conquer Europe. In 1935, Gehlen was assigned to the General Staff and began his climb upwards in the ranks, engaged first with operations and fortifications. His diligence and intelligence finally given scope for recognition, he was promoted from lieutenant to major within six years and, in 1940, was named adjutant to the chief of the General Staff and then chief of the General Staff's eastern operations division.

Gehlen had long been convinced that Germany was destined to conquer Russia and establish a well-ordered, prosperous, Berlin-dominated *Pax Germanicus* over all of Central and Eastern Europe. This belief, buttressed by contempt for Russian Communism, which he held responsible for divisive radical movements in Germany after the First World War, had led him to a thorough study of Soviet affairs. His expertise in this area led, in turn, to his appointment in 1942 as head of the General Staff's 'Foreign Armies East' division — in effect, he became director of German intelligence operations against Russia.

Over the next three years, during which he rose to the rank of brigadier general, Gehlen meticulously built an intelligence gathering service through which he was able to compile a reasonably accurate assessment of Soviet military organization, strength and deployment. Through interrogation of prisoners, front line observers, and agents planted in Moscow and elsewhere behind Russian lines, he was able also to compose a comprehensive picture of the Soviet governmental structure and of Russian economic capacities and resources.

Along with several other senior German officials, Gehlen was convinced that dissatisfaction with the Communist regime was so widespread in the Soviet Union — where Communism had been unable to overcome widespread poverty and where official terror had alienated vast segments of the population — that a campaign of psychological and political warfare would lure millions of Russians, Ukrainians and other Soviet peoples to the German side in the war. Indeed, captured Russian general Andrei Vlassov, a hero of the defence of Moscow against German attack (and later executed by the Russians), was induced to help organize and command an anti-Soviet Russian army of liberation, made up of thousands of other captured or deserted Russian soldiers who fought alongside the Germans for part of the war.

But Hitler's refusal to consider Slavs as anything more than sub-human and his sanctioning, indeed insistence upon, mass executions and other brutal treatment of Soviet peoples in German-occupied areas undermined any success this programme might have had. At the same time, Hitler's refusal to trust the accurate intelligence reports submitted by Gehlen, concerning Soviet military movements and strategic intentions, hastened the German defeat in the East. So angered was the paranoiac *Fuehrer* at increasingly pessimistic intelligence reports, as the Russians advanced on and across Germany, that Gehlen was held responsible for the news he conveyed and was dismissed from his post a month before the German surrender.

By then, he had already made plans for the future. He and his chief aides gathered their extensive files on the Soviet Union and went into hiding in the Bavarian mountains to await the arrival of the onrushing American army to whom Gehlen was prepared to offer his services and those of what could be reconstructed of his intelligence machine.

To his consternation, his offer was at first ignored. To his surprise and anger, despite the extraordinary assistance he was willing to render the Americans in the struggle against Russia (which was still America's ally), Gehlen was interned and treated as simply another high-ranking prisoner of war whose country had just perpetrated countless atrocities against civilians in its bid to conquer Europe.

Several weeks later, however, he was able to impress an astute junior American intelligence officer, engaged in interrogating prisoners to ferret out Nazi war criminals among them. Gehlen and his desire to fill American intelligence's gap in Soviet affairs were finally brought to the attention of senior United States intelligence officers.

Reports of this maverick German intelligence wizard reached Washington at a propitious moment, as far as Gehlen was concerned. They coincided with word of increasing non-cooperation by the Russians in administering conquered Germany with their western allies, and even of incidents of outright Russian hostility to western military authorities. The Iron Curtain was beginning to be lowered and the first signs of the East -West Cold War in Europe began to appear.

Under those circumstances, it seemed advisable to the Americans to give Gehlen the hearing he requested. He was flown to Washington to see exactly what services he could supply. His stature was increased by repeated requests from the Russians — who suspected that the Americans had captured the German 'Eastern Armies' intelligence chief — that he be handed over to them. Special security precautions were taken to avert a Russian kidnap attempt before he could be flown out.

In the United States, Gehlen immediately ran into strong opposition. Among American intelligence officers, some had been directly involved in tracking down those responsible for concentration camp mass murders and perpetrators of other Nazi war crimes. Some among them considered Gehlen merely another Nazi general, trying to wriggle out of responsibility for atrocities for which surviving Nazi leaders were about to be brought to trial at Nuremberg. But Gehlen was able finally to convince his interrogators in Washington that he had all along considered the Nazi crimes against civilians both morally wrong and tactically disastrous; that he had not participated in them in any way; that close friends of his had been among those who had tried to assassinate Hitler and who had been executed for the attempt; and that he could genuinely make a substantial contribution to American intelligence, particularly in view of growing Russian bellicosity.

The Agreement

Despite a tendency towards arrogance (he was later to be critical of the methods and abilities of his CIA paymasters — long before it became fashionable), Gehlen made the impression he intended to make. He knew more about Russia, its strength, political structure and resources than anyone within the then existing American intelligence system. What was more, he seemed to retain the residue of an apparatus for keeping his information up to date. By the time he had finished explaining exactly what facilities and information he could put at American disposal, he sensed that success was his and was able to insist upon his own terms for reconstructing his intelligence service in Germany. Among the provisions of the agreement he worked out with the Americans were: the new Gehlen service would work 'with' rather than under the Americans, though it would be financed by the Americans; it would not be used against German interests; it would have the option of transferring its services to a new German government when one was formed.

Agreement reached, the Americans proceeded to establish a headquarters for Gehlen and his organization, at Pullach near Munich. Already flanked by his surviving aides, Gehlen proceeded to recruit additional personnel from among former German Army colleagues and refugees from the East and to build the 'Gehlen Organization'.

It soon transpired that effective Russian counter-espionage operations had dried up most of Gehlen's sources within the Soviet Union and also constricted his operations in most of Eastern Europe. Nevertheless, in the late 1940s, this facsimile of the wartime German espionage service, with its files, evaluation bureau and residue of functioning operatives, was the most effective intelligence agency the West had operating against the Soviet Union.

Gehlen's more dramatic successes were in East Germany where many members of his wartime networks now lived and could be activated and which, together with West Germany, was rapidly becoming the major arena of East-West confrontation. Among his most notable achievements was planting his agent, Walter Gramsch, in a senior position in the East German intelligence service from which, for seven years, he fed Gehlen classified information about developments in the Soviet Zone of Germany. (To his embarrassment, the East

Germans managed to penetrate the upper reaches of the Gehlen organization as well.) Another of Gehlen's high level information sources in East Germany was Hermann Kastner, a deputy prime minister who had developed a close friendship with the Soviet military commander in East Germany but a preference for the western way of life.

During the period which encompassed the Russian blockade and attempted annexation of West Berlin in 1948 and the abortive East German uprising against the Russians in 1953, Gehlen kept the Americans informed of developments in the Soviet Zone and of Soviet installations, intentions and military movements there. The information became increasingly pertinent as the flow of East German refugees to the West became a tidal wave which endangered the East German economy and state. It compelled the Russians to scrutinize what actions they would have to take to protect their position in Eastern Europe in the light of East Germany's flounderings, and led ultimately to the building of the Berlin Wall in 1961 to save the East German Communist regime from further refugee escapes and economic disaster.

By the time the Communists constructed the wall dividing Berlin, the Gehlen organization had become a West German federal agency. In 1949, the Federal Republic of Germany had been proclaimed and in 1955 it became fully independent of the American, British and French occupying powers. The following year, the Gehlen organization was transformed into the West German intelligence service, the *Bundesnachtrichtendienst* (BND).

Anticipating as always, Gehlen had already begun spreading his wings, establishing the groundwork of a much more comprehensive national espionage service than he had operated 'with' the Americans. As a fully national operation, the BND became less exclusively involved with East German matters, though it retained an extremely active East German bureau. It revitalized operations in Russia and East Europe and began looking seriously at the Middle East, southern Europe and all other areas for which intelligence was of significance to West German policy makers.

Gehlen retired in 1968, with a parting warning that Soviet Communism remained a danger to western civilization. Fear and hatred of Communism had been the driving impulse through most of his career and had facilitated his unprecedented shift of national allegiance.

9. The Fallen Eagle

For those who need it and who are suitable candidates, a life of espionage can offer an exciting escape from a less than satisfying career. It is true that the field of spying to which, for example, a disgruntled civil servant might be assigned by foreign spy-masters is likely to be narrow. But living a daring double life, while earning clandestine gratitude and tangible rewards from flattering and sympathetic case officers, has its compensations. It can, until the spy is caught and disgraced, make up not only for the seeming futility of routine work, but also for whatever guilt feelings the personal act of treason might evoke in the recruited spy.

Stig Erik Constans Wennerstrom was at first spared feelings of guilt because his introduction to the world of spying had nothing to do with betraying Sweden, his native land, the country in which he had risen to high military rank. By the time Wennerstrom's Russian spymasters ordered him to turn his attentions to Swedish military secrets, he was too deeply involved to appreciate what was happening.

Wennerstrom was an unlikely candidate for espionage. Before being recruited by the Russians, he had reached the rank of colonel in the Swedish Air Force and was destined for important diplomatic and military assignments. His father had been a member of the Swedish Officer corps, a proud and patriotic elite against which Wennerstrom harboured no feelings of rebellion or dislike. He was paid reasonably well and was satisfied to live within his not uncomfortable means (apparently not even later extracting from the Russians as much as they offered, and were willing, to pay him). He was not a Communist and had no great fondness for Russia. Nevertheless, he served the Soviet Union faithfully for fifteen years and handed Soviet intelligence enough information to compromise Swedish military security.

His first flirtations with espionage were relatively innocent. In 1940, while Swedish air attaché in Moscow, Wennerstrom offered the Germans whatever meagre information he could gather on Russian military deployment in return for Russian secrets which the Germans acquired, which he dutifully sent back to his superiors in Stockholm. That sort of trading among diplomats is standard practice. He was simply doing his job.

After the Nazi defeat in the Second World War, the Russians seized some of the records of German military intelligence and found Wennerstrom listed as having been a source of information years before. He was then back in Stockholm, serving as an air force officer liaising with foreign air attachés, a position of considerable espionage potential. The Russians decided to determine whether his earlier trading activity with the Germans had been merely professional diplomatic behaviour or indicated that he could be recruited by them. Wennerstrom was approached by the Russian air attaché in Stockholm and asked for details of a secret Swedish military air base.

Unknowingly, the Russians had chosen a propitious moment. Wennerstrom had just been informed that his expectations and hopes of being promoted to wing commander in the Swedish Air Force had been frustrated, largely because selecting officers had decided that his skills and qualifications as a pilot did not meet their rigorous standards. It was a profound humiliation.

When the Russians approached him to test his receptivity, the prospect of redeeming himself, albeit secretly at first, flashed through Wenncrstrom's imagination. He could, he believed, penetrate the Russian intelligence service for whatever good might accrue to Sweden. He would become a double agent, working on behalf of his own country. He would not ask permission from his superiors, partly because, having just been rebuffed by them, he had no great affection for them, and partly because he was certain they would reject the daring plan which he proceeded to implement.

He told the Russians he would hand over the secrets they requested, but for a price (tacked on to discourage them from believing that he was being planted on them). The Russians happily paid up and began handling Wennerstrom with impressive tact and imagination. By the time they had finished with him, he had done exactly what he had vowed he would not do. He had become a traitor.

The Russians knew all about Wennerstrom. They knew he could not be manipulated like many western Communists who were driven by their beliefs and political commitments to obey Russian orders unquestioningly. He had to be approached roundabout. He had to be 'managed'.

Shortly after his entry into the world of espionage in Stockholm, Wennerstrom was again posted to Moscow as Swedish air attaché. He had a secret meeting there with a senior Soviet intelligence officer who made an ostentatious display of tearing up the Swedish military secrets Wennerstrom had provided to begin his charade. The fledgling double agent was assured that Russia harboured no ill-feelings against Sweden and did not really want him to provide

Swedish secrets. What the Russians wanted, Wennerstrom was told, was any information he could provide about American military forces.

Wennerstrom was relieved. He had not been comfortable with the idea of handing over Swedish secrets, no matter how meagre, even though he had believed it was necessary to do so to establish his cover as a Russian spy. He was less concerned about the task of feeding the Russians American secrets, especially as he was unlikely to gain access to many of great significance as a Swedish diplomat in Moscow. The important thing was to sustain the impression which he had given Soviet intelligence officers that he was their man. When the Russians offered him a secret but formal position in the Soviet intelligence service, Wennerstrom was flattered. It was more appreciative treatment than he had received from his Swedish superiors, and required practically nothing of him. He gratefully accepted.

During the next three years, Wennerstrom supplied the Russians with bits and pieces of information about American military equipment, deployment and planning, all of it picked up through his diplomatic and military contacts. While the military attaché of a neutral country may not have direct access to much foreign classified information, a sprinkling does come through in conversations, official visits and semi-secret literature disseminated by arms salesmen. Nevertheless, little that Wennerstrom could offer the Russians about America was very important, and most of it the Russians knew already. However, he was treated by his controllers in Moscow as if he were making unprecedented contributions to Soviet defences. He was told, and believed, that because of the secrets he had acquired and passed on, Soviet air defences had been reorganized in such a way that a previously possible American sneak attack, which would have started World War

Three, was now out of the question.

The Swedish colonel was given the rank of major general in Soviet intelligence, to show exactly how much his espionage activities were appreciated. To gild the lily, the man Swedish Air Force examiners had considered not good enough as a pilot, was given the Russian codename, *The Eagle.*

Beginning in Earnest

Earlier in his career, Wennerstrom had been in close contact with American Air Force officers with whom he had met socially and traded bits of information. The Russians had known of this for some time, but when Wennerstrom, to their great pleasure, was transferred from Moscow and assigned to be Swedish air attaché in Washington, they summoned him to a secret meeting place outside Moscow to chastise him. They told him that they had just learned that he had also worked with the American CIA — which was not true but which Wennerstrom, recalling his exchanges with American officers, was prepared to believe. The Russians said this was a serious offence for a man who was now a senior Soviet officer, but in view of the good work he had done for them and his obvious sincerity, they were prepared to overlook it. What was more, they wanted him to resume his contacts with American intelligence, if the opportunity presented itself in Washington, and report back on developments.

Now a fully committed Soviet agent, and having long forgotten his intention of using the position to serve Sweden, Wennerstrom was relieved and grateful, two feelings the Russians repeatedly induced in him. They played him like a delicate violin and he responded perfectly in tune.

He was in Washington for five years (1952/57), during which time he dispatched a substantial quantity of information to Moscow. As air attaché of a country in the market for American-made defence equipment, and as chief Swedish Air

Force purchasing agent in the United States, he was warmly welcomed at aircraft factories and air bases. He received stacks of literature from the Pentagon merely by asking for it. 'I had,' he said later, 'entrée everywhere.' He gathered information on aircraft, guided missiles, computers and a wide variety of military goods. As an honoured member of the Washington diplomatic corps, he was also able to gather details on technological developments in other fields, including atomic energy.

He was directly controlled by a case officer working out of the Soviet embassy in Washington to whom he handed his information, usually directly. There was nothing unusual about foreign diplomats meeting in their offices, or for lunch, or going out for a drink together. Once, Wennerstrom said, he even handed over photographs of secret documents to a Russian diplomat in the Pentagon itself.

Despite routine denials from American intelligence, it is probable that this respected and liked Swedish air attaché, with his outspoken pro-American sentiments, was able to acquire and transmit information of value to the Russians. But it is also likely that, as in Moscow, much of what he passed on was available to the Russians from other sources. It seems probable that, at this stage, Wennerstrom was still being groomed for his most important assignment, which began when he returned to Sweden from Washington in 1957, bringing with him an Order of the Legion of Merit, awarded to him by the United States for his contribution to Swedish American relations.

Back in Stockholm, Wennerstrom was appointed chief of the air section of the Swedish Defence Ministry's command office. His instructions from the Russians were to feed information on American equipment used in Swedish defence operations. This was the job for which the Russians intended him when he was first recruited. Aside from the fact that much of the key apparatus in Swedish defence installations was of American manufacture, it was virtually impossible to report on parts of the defence edifice without overlapping into other parts, until finally the entire set-up could be pieced together.

Above suspicion, Wennerstrom was in a position to record everything to which he could gain access and which might be of the slightest interest to Soviet intelligence. Unchallenged, he took home documents to photograph and kept so busy that his Russian contact in Stockholm was hard pressed to keep up with him, to maintain security for transmissions for Moscow and to obtain enough microfilm to keep Wennerstrom supplied.

It took the Swedish authorities another five years to catch up with *The Eagle,* by which time he occupied an exalted position at the Swedish Foreign Office — adviser on disarmament questions. Swedish security had noted years before that he had been particularly friendly with the Soviet air attaché in Stockholm, the man who first recruited him. The fact was noted in a file and put aside. In 1959, he visited Amsterdam under circumstances which a colleague travelling with him considered peculiar — a seemingly unplanned jaunt during a plane stopover. Hearing of it, Swedish security made a routine check of his office and found a handbook of photography; not particularly suspicious, but that fact went into the file too, as did a report that Wennerstrom's car was spotted near a place which Swedish counter-intelligence believed to be used by the Russians for clandestine contact.

There was, however, still no conclusive evidence that Wennerstrom was a spy, though there was enough suspicion to keep him from getting a job for which he had applied, the Swedish Air Force general staff. There also seemed sufficient grounds for tapping his phone. Suspicious conversations were overheard — one, between Wennerstrom and a Russian diplomat, convoluted enough to sound like a coded exchange; another in which Wennerstrom's daughter told a friend about her father's high-powered radio which she was forbidden to use. A detailed check revealed that Wennerstrom had been taking large amounts of secret documents from the Defence Ministry and related offices, ostensibly to work on at home. A woman who worked as a part-time maid for the Wennerstroms was interrogated and told of his locked study, the visit of Russians, suspicious rolls of film, and her own belief that there were unanswered questions about Wennerstrom's behaviour. The discreet acquisition from Wennerstrom's home of film of classified documents overcame any remaining doubts that he was a spy.

The arrest was as low-keyed and dramatic as a Swedish art film. Wennerstrom drove to work one morning, parked his car near his office and started across a bridge to his office building. Unmarked cars moved into place to block both sides of the bridge. A security officer then approached Wennerstrom and took him into custody.

At first, he vigorously denied being a spy, but confessed when confronted with the evidence which an intensive search of his house had uncovered — documents, microfilm, code books, a short wave radio, a stack of money which Wennerstrom finally conceded had come from the Russians. An attempt at suicide in jail failed. The man who had hoped to serve his country by tricking the Russians was sentenced to life imprisonment, a sentence which was later to be reduced as *The Eagle* grew old.

10. GUERRILLA WARFARE

The term guerrilla warfare applies to a type of combat
involving the use of irregular methods of battle. In times of
war, regular military units (sometimes deployed by national
espionage services) as well as partisan forces have employed
guerrilla tactics against an enemy. In situations of non-military
belligerence, such as the Cold War or the Russian-Chinese
rivalry, national espionage services have often sought to
exploit, for their own purposes, the actions and goals of
guerrillas in third countries, outside the context of direct
hostility.

Few cases so graphically illustrate the recurring link
between guerrilla warfare and espionage operations in non-war
circumstances as the development of confrontation in Angola
in 1975 when the Portuguese precipitously withdrew from
control of that mineral-rich former colony. Russian agents
busily supplied and trained the forces of one guerrilla
movement, the Popular Movement for the Liberation of
Angola (MPLA). At the same time, Chinese agents were
'advising' a rival guerrilla movement, the National Liberation
Front of Angola (FNLA). The Russian objective was control
of Angola by the pro-Communist MPLA. The Chinese, more
troubled by Russian expansion than about the possibility of a
Communist defeat in the Angola contest, were determined to
prevent Moscow from emerging with its influence and prestige
in Africa enhanced.

To extend national spheres of influence and/or limit those
of adversary nations is a standing assignment for all major

espionage services. The use of foreign guerrilla movements as instruments in pursuing this objective has long been common. Lawrence of Arabia intensified an Arab desert rebellion against Turkish rulers in the First World War and, thereby, furthered British interests in the Middle East. As they swept across the Pacific in the Second World War, the Japanese supported anti-American guerrillas in the Philippines and anti-Dutch guerrillas in what was later to be Indonesia. During the 1960s and early 1970s, Cuban agents were deployed with guerrilla movements in many parts of Latin America to help them try to undermine both existing governments and the influence of the United States in that part of the world. The Russians also financed and supported a desert guerrilla war against the Sultan of Oman in a bid to acquire coastal influence in the strategic Arabian Sea.

In recent years, a new form of guerrilla warfare has evolved, that practised by so-called urban guerrillas. Politically motivated groups have launched sporadic 'revolutionary' raids on normally secure elements of society. In Argentina, guerrillas dynamited a warship being outfitted at a shipyard and murdered political opponents. In England, Irish Republican Army 'soldiers' planted bombs in pubs and other buildings and shot down members of security forces. American 'Weathermen' detonated a bomb in New York City police headquarters and in banks in other American cities. Individuals were kidnapped and held for ransom. Sniping attacks were launched on police.

In Communist and other totalitarian countries, espionage services, through tradition and orientation, already concentrated effectively on domestic security problems. Elsewhere, the growth of politically-inspired terrorism became an urgent national and international concern. It appeared to be an epidemic which crossed national frontiers and oceanic barriers. It made enormous demands on many governments, sometimes outstripping police control capabilities. In some cases, political terrorism posed greater threats to governments and social order than did external adversaries and, consequently, compelled the attention of national intelligence services.

The 1968 student rebellion in Paris precipitated the departure of President Charles de Gaulle from public office. The repertoire of the Uruguayan Tupamaros encompassed political kidnapping (including British ambassador Geoffrey Jackson), political murder (including American security adviser Dan Mitrione), and the temporary seizure of hinterland areas as muscle-flexing exercises. The Quebec Liberation Front engaged in a series of bombings and bank robberies and murdered a Quebec minister in its campaign to gain independence for French-speaking regions of Canada. Japanese terrorists armed themselves with helmets, gas masks, shields and staves and rushed into open combat with the police for control of the streets. Palestinian terrorists hijacked and blew up planes and murdered the Prime Minister of Jordan, the American ambassador to Sudan and Israeli athletes at the 1972 Munich Olympics when their more conventional guerrilla attacks on Israel failed to gain restoration of Arab control of Palestine. Nihilists ranged across West Germany, robbing and killing in an orgy of violence designed to undermine the existing framework of West German society.

The Brazilian, Carlos Marighella, one of the philosophers of urban terrorism, shot dead by Brazilian police in 1969, outlined the goals of urban guerrillas. Their purpose, he said, was to transform a political context, which inhibited the 'revolution', into a military context in which the authorities would be compelled to resort to intolerably extreme measures to combat terrorism. Social order would be shattered and the conditions for revolution would emerge. Urban guerrillas were, in effect, to be provocateurs, goading the authorities into such repressive security operations that the general populace would be penalized, resentful and, ultimately, rebellious.

IRA operations in Northern Ireland were often designed to provoke a massive response by British troops in Catholic districts, thus enraging otherwise peaceful Catholics and transforming them into IRA recruits. Eritrean guerrillas, seeking independence from Ethiopia for their province, succeeded, through sniping at and openly assaulting Ethiopian military units, in provoking such savage indiscriminate reprisals against Eritrean civilians that Ethiopia was reduced to holding on to Eritrea exclusively by force of arms.

Traditional nationalist guerrilla campaigns suggest an obvious, though rarely simple, response. To succeed, counterinsurgency operations must be devised to isolate, undercut and overwhelm the insurgents in their chosen field of battle without alienating those the insurgents seek to win over. This was done successfully by the British against Communist guerrillas in what is now Malaysia and failed in American operations against Communists in South Vietnam.

However, urban guerrillas present different dimensions to the problem of counter-insurgency. Their chosen field of battle could be the busy main street of a nation's capital, crowded with innocent people; or it might be in another country, beyond the jurisdiction and conventional powers of a nation's security forces. Those involved in urban guerrilla operations may be foreign nationals, difficult to detect or apprehend. Latin Americans from many countries, easily disguisable as foreign tourists, were enrolled by the Tupamaros in Uruguay. A Japanese 'Red Army' suicide squad, operating on behalf of Palestinian guerrillas, gunned down tourists (many of them Puerto Rican Christian pilgrims) at an Israeli airport. The

Palestinians, Cubans, and North Koreans, as well as Russians and Chinese, are known to operate guerrilla training schools for foreign revolutionaries.

To meet the challenge of urban guerrillas, intelligence services in the United States, Western Europe, Japan, Latin America and other countries, united in a fraternity of mutual interest, have attempted to establish lines of communication through which to exchange information on known guerrilla organizations, operations and objectives. Some of this information has been acquired through penetration agents planted in guerrilla groups, but success along those lines has been marginal. Greater, but still limited success was achieved by the exchange of information on known terrorists, identified through previous arrest or operations. (Palestinian and Japanese guerrillas took to concealing their faces with masks or scarves in hijack and hostage-taking missions during which their identities might have been revealed and recorded for their future capture.)

Despite the successes of many traditional-style guerrilla movements, the urban guerrillas have consistently failed to achieve their ultimate objectives, though they have often inflicted serious damage and aroused official anxiety. The reason for their failure is not hard to decipher. Invariably, the urban guerrillas have had only meagre links, or no links at all, with sufficiently potent potential revolutionary elements in society — whether the working classes, the army or the peasantry in their target countries. In many places, most urban guerrillas have had middle class origins and upbringing, giving the impression of 'slumming' for excitement. One American pundit has suggested that the urban guerrilla movement in the United States and some other countries was the only revolutionary conspiracy in history financed by momma.

11.   INDUSTRIAL ESPIONAGE

A few years ago, an extraordinary incident took place at New York's Kennedy Airport. A man occupying a cubicle of an airport men's room took off his trousers, stuffed $20,000 he had been instructed to bring with him into their pockets, and passed the trousers under the partition to an adjoining cubicle. Another man waiting there, who had given the unexpected trouser-stripping command, extracted the money from the pockets, replaced it with some documents, returned the trousers over the partition and fled before they could be put on again.

The plan had been designed to guarantee his escape, but he did not get far. The police were waiting to take him into custody for engaging in the fastest expanding corner of the world of spying — industrial espionage. The arrested man, a junior executive of a pharmaceutical company, had tried to sell details of his firm's new, still-secret toothpaste (about to be launched with a lavishly financed advertising campaign) to a rival company. The rival firm pretended to play along, but arranged for the transaction to be monitored and for the toothpaste spy to be apprehended.

Against his failure, however, can be measured the increasing number of successes industrial spies have racked up in recent years. A disgruntled employee of the Cyanamid Pharmaceutical Company of America sold secrets of a new antibiotic to an Italian drug firm. Cyanamid had already spent thirty million dollars on research for the drug and probably also lost about three times as much in sales as a result of the theft. Photographs of a new model Mercedes Benz car were illicitly acquired and published, inflicting a severe financial wound upon the manufacturers when cancellation orders for soon-to-be-outdated Mercedes models began flooding in. A British manufacturer of electric light bulbs, about to launch a new model neon tube, suddenly found itself in competition with a company founded by former employees who had worked on developing the tube.

No company with secrets to hide — involving finances, products or marketing — can feel secure any longer from the probability that someone is trying to steal them. A state of business siege has been established in which it is believed — not without reason — that even the walls have ears and that reports on confidential business meetings could be dropped on the desks of competitors within hours.

Included in the information commonly sought by the growing corps of industrial spies are details of new products and production methods, planned advertising campaigns and pricing policies, such major company changes as mergers and take-overs in prospect, such company problems as executive rivalries and prospective strikes, and the identity and reliability of raw material sources.

Among major targets for industrial spies are also the deliberations of merchant banks which can influence the operations of entire industries. Among specific chemical formulae sought are those for tranquillizers, perfume essences, insect repellents and other products with vast potential markets. It is common knowledge that among those who attend fashion previews in Paris and other major cities are many who rush back to hotel rooms or nearby cafes to sketch from memory the fashions which have just been paraded before them, details of which are then fed to selected garment manufacturers around the world who, without charge or delay, can 'follow' the lead of expensive trend-setting designers.

For many years, Japanese industrial spies — they considered themselves merely resourceful businessmen — converged on major western cities to study new developments in photographic equipment, radio and television receivers and other areas of expanding consumer interest. The result was a flood of incomparably inexpensive models, based on American and European designs, produced by Japan's soon-to-vanish cheap labour economy.

The incidents of industrial espionage which come to light are a small fraction of the number that actually take place. Neither the spies engaged in stealing industrial and business secrets, nor the companies whose competitive positions are damaged, nor the firms which benefit from the pilfered information are anxious for word to get around. But, in fact, industrial espionage has reached epidemic proportions. It has developed into a major concern for business organizations and they have responded by spending huge sums to combat the menace.

There has been widespread tightening of company security. Company payrolls have been extended to take on security specialists. In view of the increased use of electronic eavesdropping equipment, executive offices and boardrooms of large firms are now regularly 'swept' for bugs. Nevertheless, there remains a great number of people in the business, finance and research communities who are willing to pay a price for someone else's confidential information. The prevailing climate was best described by an American business executive who contended recently that it is no longer simply ethical to steal business secrets; it is obligatory. Security operation have managed to seal off only the most obvious and lockable leaks.

Types of Spies

There are many varieties of industrial spies. They include shrewd businessmen, like the Japanese of the 1950s and 1960s, who copy successful products and market them cheaply enough to undercut original designs. They also include knowledge-merchants, people who, in the normal course of their work, acquire business secrets which can be sold - disgruntled or hard-pressed employees, former employees starting businesses of their own, contented employees lured away from their jobs by 'headhunting' rival companies, and temporary employees (like secretary 'temps') who have no allegiance to their employers but who may pick up bits of valuable information.

Though obtaining monetary reward for the secrets they acquire, these are really the amateurs of the industrial espionage world. The true professionals are those whose full time trade is seeking business secrets either for clients or on 'spec'. Even honest businessmen may be sorely tempted to pay what's asked for information that could materially benefit their companies, and even save them from bankruptcy.

The Living Legend Lives

The tremendous upsurge in industrial espionage has revived the fortunes of one of the living legends of modern society — the private detective. Now equipped with a galaxy of gadgets, many 'private eyes' have profitably immersed themselves in business spying, while others have joined the growing army of company security officers.

Like strategic espionage, industrial spying and related practices have a venerable history. In the sixth century, two monks commissioned by Emperor Justinian smuggled silk worm eggs out of China and brought them back to Constantinople to launch the silk growing industry in the west. More recently, a nineteenth century British businessman and adventurer secretly removed rubber plant seeds from Brazil, sneaking them past customs inspectors, and brought them back to England from which rubber trees, which grew from the seeds under controlled conditions, were dispatched to Ceylon, Borneo and Malaya (all then part of the British Empire) to found vast rubber plantations there.

But the physical acquisition of tangible material has always been on the periphery of industrial espionage. The major objective has been what the American Society for Industrial Security described as the 'elusive, intangible commodity knowledge'. The focus has always been the acquisition of industrial intelligence.

The business spy once had to rely on informants. But he now has a selection of electronic aides, eavesdropping mechanisms of increasingly sophisticated design. These days, bugs for recording or transmitting confidential discussions can be planted just about anywhere in offices and boardrooms. Miniature microphones have been disguised as tie clips and cigarette lighters, clipped onto ear hooks of eyeglass frames, concealed in wristwatches and fitted into attaché cases. There are sensitive listening devices for hearing conversations through walls. There is a gadget for transforming a pre-planted 'infinity' bug in an office telephone into a transmitter, activated by dialling the telephone number, even from thousands of miles away. The victim's telephone will not ring and his receiver may not even be lifted from its cradle, but the eavesdropper — far, far away — will, through his own telephone, hear everything that is said in the bugged office.

Vans, kitted out like spy trawlers, can be parked in the street to pick up, with some degree of selectivity, telephone calls being made in the immediate area. 'Night sight' photography is now available to the better equipped industrial spy, enabling him to photograph documents in company offices or laboratories at night without attracting attention by turning on lights.

The possibilities for electronic spying are dazzling, particularly with the increased use of computers in business activity. A remote spy computer can be 'locked' on to the computer of a company that's being raided. It can extract virtually any information the victimized computer contains and even give it a limited range of false instructions to alter its information banks to the advantage of rival companies or individuals.

Strenuous efforts are now being made to 'spy-proof' computers. As with other kinds of espionage, industrial spying is engaged in a seemingly endless cycle of innovations to make the acquisition of secrets both easier and more difficult.

Printed in Great Britain
by Amazon